Birds&Blooms
Backyard Basics

Female tiger
swallowtail on
woodland phlox

A *Birds & Blooms* Book

© 2022 RDA Enthusiast
Brands, LLC.
1610 N. 2nd St., Suite 102,
Milwaukee, WI 53212-3906

ISBN:
978-1-62145-877-7
(Hardcover)
978-1-62145-878-4
(Paperback)
978-1-62145-895-1
(Epub)

Component Number:
118500112H

We are committed to both
the quality of our products
and the service we provide
to our customers. We value
your comments, so please
feel free to contact us at
*TMBBookTeam@
TrustedMediaBrands.com*.

For more *Birds & Blooms*
products, visit us at
our website: *www.
birdsandblooms.com*.

Text, photography and
illustrations for *Backyard
Basics* are based on articles
previously published in *Birds
& Blooms* magazine (*www.
birdsandblooms.com*).

Hardcover printed in the United
States of America
10 9 8 7 6 5 4 3 2 1

Paperback printed in China
10 9 8 7 6 5 4 3 2 1

KEVIN COLLISON / SHUTTERSTOCK

Table of Contents

ON THE FRONT COVER
Downy woodpecker
Photo by Marie Read

ON THE TITLE PAGE
Blue jay
Photo by Marie Read

Yellow-
rumped
warbler

White cleome

Welcome!

Why do birds migrate? What is this mystery plant? How can I attract pollinators to my yard? Get answers to everything you've ever needed to know about birds, butterflies and plants from your *Birds & Blooms* experts, Kimberly and Kenn Kaufman and Melinda Myers. Packed with beautiful photography and loads of practical advice and simple solutions, this special-edition book features more than 300 answers to must-know reader questions. Including common dilemmas and head-scratching curiosities, *Backyard Basics* is essential for any backyard gardener or birding enthusiast!

—THE EDITORS OF
BIRDS & BLOOMS MAGAZINE

MEET THE EXPERTS

Kimberly and Kenn Kaufman are the duo behind the *Kaufman Field Guide* series. They lead bird trips and speak all over the world.

Melinda Myers is a nationally known, award-winning garden expert, TV/radio host and author of more than 20 books.

CHAPTER 1

Bird Behavior

With curious antics and unusual feeding patterns, birds keep us guessing about what they'll do next. Learn the why, what and how behind some of their most head-scratching high jinks.

Q Blue jays are pecking at the spindles on my wraparound porch. What can I do to stop them?

Kimberly Williams BELCHERTOWN, MASSACHUSETTS

Kenn and Kimberly: Paint in light colors often contains limestone, a source of calcium. Some birds—particularly blue jays—seek out calcium as a needed supplement, especially during the breeding season. They've even been known to cache calcium in other seasons for use during breeding. To discourage this unwelcome alteration to your porch, try offering the birds some eggshells, giving them an easier (and less destructive) source of calcium. Be sure to sterilize the eggshells first by either boiling them for five minutes, or heating them in the oven for 30 minutes at 250 degrees Fahrenheit.

Did You Know?
Blue jays often build their nests 10 to 25 feet high in the outer branches of trees.

Q Hummingbirds visit my feeders every day, year-round. Where do they sleep at night in chilly weather, and how do they survive the cold?

Kay Teseniar KELSO, WASHINGTON

Kenn and Kimberly: Hummingbirds will often find a twig that's sheltered from the wind to rest on for the night. Also, in winter they can enter a deep sleeplike state known as torpor. All body functions slow dramatically; metabolism drops by as much as 95% and heart rate and body temperature decline significantly. Torpor lets hummingbirds conserve precious energy and survive surprisingly low temperatures. In spite of their fragile appearance, they're tough little critters!

Did You Know?
You often see orioles feeding on oranges and grape jelly, but they also eat insects.

Q Baltimore orioles disappear from my feeders for several weeks, come back and then leave again. They keep this up all summer. Why is this?

Marjorie Moe DECORAH, IOWA

Kenn and Kimberly: One possible explanation is that the size of their territory can vary during the season. A male Baltimore oriole will defend a larger territory by driving away other males while he's trying to attract a mate. Later, after he's paired up and the female has laid eggs, the size of the defended territory becomes smaller and centered around the nest. At that stage, orioles will roam outside their defended areas to visit food sources in the surrounding neighborhood. If you don't have a pair of orioles nesting nearby, several oriole pairs might be stopping by, but not on a regular schedule.

Backyard Tip

Orioles also like nectar. Buy a special oriole feeder and fill it with sugar water, just as you would for hummingbirds.

Q We put out grape jelly for the orioles, but the robins find it, too, and dive-bomb the orioles. This keeps the orioles away. Any suggestions?

Dennis Ruzicka
HUTCHINSON, MINNESOTA

Kenn and Kimberly: It's hard for us to think about ways to discourage robins because we enjoy them so much, but we understand the desire to keep orioles coming to your feeders. Since orioles are the smaller and more agile of the two birds, consider placing the jelly container in a fly-through-style feeder to make it harder for the robins to feed. Or add extra jelly stations spaced far enough apart to feed both the orioles and the robins.

Q I spotted this downy woodpecker on the side of my sugar maple tree. It had its head turned and tucked into its wings as if it was sleeping. What was it doing?

Larry Barger HAMILTON, OHIO

Kenn and Kimberly: The bird appears to be taking a short nap. When downy woodpeckers go to sleep for the night, they usually escape to a tree cavity. But sometimes, even midday, a woodpecker may fall asleep for a short time while clinging to a tree trunk. It does this by bracing against the tree with stiff tail feathers and locking its toes onto the bark.

Q We live in the Poconos, and last winter we saw a robin eating suet. We've been feeding the birds for 35 years and have never seen this before. Can you tell us why?

JoAnn Bender GOULDSBORO, PENNSYLVANIA

Kenn and Kimberly: American robins have a varied diet, eating anything from worms and other invertebrates to many kinds of berries and other small fruits. In winter, when the rest of their food is tough to find, their focus shifts to fruit. When their natural food supply is depleted, birds will take advantage of whatever they can find. Individuals within a species vary in their eating habits, so not all robins will come to suet. But yours was adaptable enough to make good use of this nutritious treat.

Did You Know?
You may not see robins much in winter because they're concentrated in places with lots of wild berries.

Q Why do robins eat only worms from the lawn? I never see them at my bird feeders, which exclusively contain black oil sunflower seeds.

Pat Schulthies LOYSVILLE, PENNSYLVANIA

Kenn and Kimberly: Robins primarily eat invertebrates, such as earthworms, beetle grubs, grasshoppers and caterpillars. They also eat a variety of fruits and berries. Because seeds aren't part of an American robin's usual diet, you need to be creative with your offerings. To attract robins to your feeders, try live mealworms along with a variety of fruits and berries, such as blueberries, apple halves and grapes. Robins also love water, so a water feature is a smart way to bring them to your feeding station.

Q A robin attacks our car and flies into our sunroom windows. What causes this behavior, and what should we do?

Craig Carty
MOUNTAIN HOME, ARKANSAS

Kenn and Kimberly: At certain times of year, robins, cardinals and other birds are very territorial. They mistake their reflection for another bird and will launch repeated attacks to drive the "intruder" away. The only truly effective way to discourage these attacks is to eliminate the reflection until the bird loses interest. Cover your car mirrors with small garbage bags, securing them with rubber bands. For your sunroom windows, try hanging sheets of dark plastic, newspaper or old sheets on the outside of the window. Or rub soap on the outside of the window where the robin usually attacks. Either approach should do the trick and keep your robins safe.

Q If the ground is still frozen, what do hungry robins eat?

Judy Schmidt WEST BEND, IOWA

Kenn and Kimberly: Although robins are very conspicuous when they go hunting for earthworms on open lawns, worms make up only a small portion of their diet year-round. In winter, flocks of robins seek out small fruits and berries, supplementing them with any insects they find. After the ground thaws in spring, we'll start to see robins out on those lawns again, running and pausing as they search for juicy earthworms.

Q Woodpeckers drill on our windows. We've tried hanging CDs as well as motion-activated spiders. The spiders seem to work best; however, they are not 100 percent effective. Do you have any other helpful suggestions?

Lynn Meyer CEDAR CREEK, TEXAS

Kenn and Kimberly: Woodpeckers use drumming as a form of communication. Surfaces like windows, tin roofs and aluminum siding provide great amplification, so they often attract these feathered percussionists. Discouraging them can be a challenge, but you're on the right track. Any item that moves or flutters makes a good deterrent, and reflective streamers are the most effective. One DIY approach is to cut a Mylar balloon or aluminum foil into thin streamers, tape them to a dowel rod and attach the whole thing to the top of your window. Some homeowners have had success providing alternative surfaces to lure woodpeckers away from their house by fastening a section of metal roofing to a post.

LEFT TO RIGHT: CAROL L. EDWARDS; JAMES PIERCE/SHUTTERSTOCK; DON JOHNSTON/ALL CANADA PHOTOS

Q. In early spring, my oriole feeder was busy every day. Then the activity abruptly stopped. I know when the eggs hatch, the birds stop coming to the feeder, but will return. When can I expect them to come back?

Donna Wolfe GOODRICH, MICHIGAN

Kenn and Kimberly: You're not alone in trying to solve this mystery. With so many people feeding orioles these days, we get this question a lot. The answer is nestled in their beautifully woven hanging nest. Yep, it's about raising the kids! During the breeding season, orioles focus on more protein-rich food, foraging mostly for insects to feed their young. But once the young orioles have fledged, the parents frequently bring them to visit feeders. We suggest that you keep tabs on when they disappear, give it three to four weeks, and begin offering food again. You may be rewarded with visits from the parents and the youngsters!

14 BACKYARD BASICS

Q I noticed blue jays chasing away crows in my backyard. What threat do the crows pose for the jays?

Carol Mudd SAINT JOHNS, FLORIDA

Kenn and Kimberly: It's true that crows do sometimes take eggs or nestlings out of the nests of smaller birds, so jays and other birds are sometimes agitated when there are crows around. Blue jays are also sort of ornery birds. They're intelligent, have a lot of energy, and will sometimes harass hawks or crows for no obvious reason—they seem to be doing it just for fun.

Q I have had black-capped chickadees in my yard every day for more than 25 years and suddenly they've disappeared. Can you explain this?

Judith Bazinet NORWICH, CONNECTICUT

Kenn and Kimberly: It's hard to say without knowing your local situation, but there are some possible reasons why your chickadees might have disappeared. A chickadee flock will range over an area of several acres. Even if the habitat in your yard is still good for them, changes in the surrounding neighborhood (like the removal of too many trees) could make the area less suitable. Also, chickadee population numbers may rise and fall, and your local population might have hit a low point. If that's the case, their numbers should start to rebound within a year or two, as long as good habitat is available.

Backyard Tip

Attract chickadees with feeders full of peanuts and sunflower seeds. They'll also stop for suet!

Expert Foragers
Downies have smaller bills than other woodpeckers, but their bills are still useful tools for plucking bugs out from under tree bark.

Q My husband worries about woodpeckers in the area. Do they damage trees?

Beth Pearson
PAULINE, SOUTH CAROLINA

Kenn and Kimberly: It's completely understandable to be concerned about these industrious birds hacking away but, in reality, woodpeckers almost never damage healthy trees. In fact, they usually protect them by eating insects that would otherwise attack the tree. Woodpeckers typically excavate their nest holes in trees or limbs that already are dead or that have internal issues like heartwood rot. When a woodpecker digs out a big section of living trunk or branch, it's going after insects, such as beetle grubs or carpenter ants that already are damaging the tree. So attracting woodpeckers won't put your treescape at any risk.

Backyard Tip
Look for cedar waxwings in flocks this winter, especially if you've got berry trees nearby. These birds spend most of the year together.

Q Besides starlings and Canada geese, what other birds fly in flocks? I have recently noticed that I don't see others, such as doves, blue jays, etc., in large flocks.

Debby Rinehart TALBOTT, TENNESSEE

Kenn and Kimberly: While there are some birds that are truly solitary—the great horned owl, peregrine falcon and solitary sandpiper, for example—many birds are social only at certain times of the year. Quite a few species, including some that are often considered solitary, form flocks during migration. Blue jays, flickers, robins, swallows and a few species of hawks are examples. Blackbirds and waterfowl are among the birds that may be in flocks most of the time when they're not actively nesting.

A male purple finch perches in a flowering crabapple tree.

Q Purple finches chew my Sedum spectabile plants bare. Is this behavior normal?

Rick Duba APPLETON, WISCONSIN

Kenn and Kimberly: I have seen birds pluck leaves and flowers off this and other plants. I assume they use them for nesting, or in some cases, food. Birds may forage elsewhere if you cover the plant as soon as it sprouts, before damage begins. After a while, you may be able to lift the cover and enjoy a clear view of your sedum.

Q Two young downy woodpeckers visited my sugar-water feeder several times a day. Small hummingbirds had a tough time chasing them away. Is it common for woodpeckers to sip sugar water?

Bernard Dudek
DOWNERS GROVE, ILLINOIS

Kenn and Kimberly: Hummingbirds and orioles aren't the only birds with a hankering for nectar or sugar water. Some woodpeckers like it, too. This is especially true for red-bellied, golden-fronted and Gila woodpeckers, which have quite varied diets. Downy woodpeckers also partake of the sweet stuff, so it's no surprise that they'll take advantage of an easy source like a hummingbird feeder when they find one. We suggest that you invest in another feeder for the woodpeckers if they're discouraging your other birds from feeding.

Q I noticed a few birds sitting around the birdbath with their tails resting in the water. Why would that be?

Bill Bellairs OXFORD, MICHIGAN

Kenn and Kimberly: Usually there's a good reason for the things that birds do, but in this case, it's just a coincidence. They couldn't cool themselves by sticking their tails into the water—the tails consist of nothing but feathers and have no nerve endings. So if they have the tail tips underwater, it's just a result of the position that they happen to be in at the moment.

A thirsty downy woodpecker sips from a feeder filled with sugar water.

Keep It Clear
When making sugar water from scratch, skip the red food coloring. The dye may be harmful to birds, and it's completely unnecessary.

Q Usually, Steller's jays and western scrub-jays come and gobble up peanuts I put out. Since late summer, they have not come at all for anything. Why have they not visited?

Justus Morales PINE MOUNTAIN CLUB, CALIFORNIA

Kenn and Kimberly: There are many potential reasons why your jays are forsaking you. Jays are in the corvid family, known as one of the most intelligent of all bird families. It's possible that a hawk or another predator chased them away from the feeders and now they're reluctant to take the risk. Another possibility is that the birds are finding natural food more plentiful at this time of year and aren't as interested in your offerings. You might also check to make sure that there aren't roaming cats in the area, which can be a major deterrent to birds at feeders.

Steller's jay

Q I really enjoy photographing birds, but sometimes they seem scared of my camera. Do the sounds or flashes bother them?

Gianna Williams MAYFIELD, NEW YORK

Kenn and Kimberly: Individual birds react differently to cameras. Some are startled by any kind of sound or flash, and others seem to ignore them completely. If possible, it's good to use a telephoto lens or superzoom camera so you can stay back and take photos from a distance. Sometimes a flash is helpful, and a high-quality flash will be adjustable so that you can use just enough light to fill in shadows. That's much better than blasting the birds with bright light: It doesn't disturb them as much, and it makes for more pleasing images.

Q A ruby-throated hummingbird and titmouse looked like they were playing tag in my backyard. What were they doing?

Tom Balkwill LITHIA, FLORIDA

Kenn and Kimberly: We sometimes see hummingbirds that appear to be chasing small songbirds, like goldfinches or warblers. It's fascinating, and we don't completely know why it happens. Hummingbirds sometimes aggressively defend their favorite flowers or feeders from other hummers, but a songbird wouldn't be competing for those food sources, so there's no reason to chase them. The best explanation we can offer is that birds have individual personalities, and some hummingbirds are just extra feisty, chasing other birds to burn off all that energy.

Marsh Singers?

Listen for male red-winged blackbirds in wetland areas. They perch on tall vegetation, and belt out *conk-la-ree!*

Q Why do birds sing after a storm?

Lori Sheldon BORGER, TEXAS

Kenn and Kimberly: After a storm, especially a bad one, it's reassuring to hear birds singing. It's mostly male birds that sing. They tune up after storms for the same reasons that they belt out songs early in the morning. Each male sings to announce his claim to a territory—the area that he defends for raising a family—and to communicate with his mate. So at dawn's first light, or as soon as the storm passes, the message in his song is "I'm still here." It reassures his mate that he's guarding the territory and lets neighboring males know that this turf is still occupied.

Feeding Time
A pileated parent feeds one of his young, who will stay in the nest for almost a month.

Q. I often see comments from people who are surprised to see pileated woodpeckers. Are they rare? I have three that visit my backyard suet feeder daily.

Ramona Anaya ALGER, MICHIGAN

Kenn and Kimberly: Pileated woodpeckers had become rare in many areas during past centuries when forests were being cut down on a large scale. In recent decades they have made a good comeback. However, they still require some kind of forest cover with big trees, so they don't appear in most people's yards. Even when they live close to people, it seems to take a while for pileated woodpeckers to become accustomed to bird feeders. You are lucky to have them as regular visitors!

Did You Know?
Cardinals aren't picky. They eat fruit, seeds, peanuts, corn, insects and even suet.

Q A male northern cardinal loves our hanging suet. We thought cardinals were primarily ground feeders. Is this normal?
Bill Roberts HUDSON, NEW HAMPSHIRE

Kenn and Kimberly: While dangling cardinals aren't all that common, we do see this happen from time to time. There are several possible explanations. Cardinals show a strong affinity for sunflower and safflower seeds. If your suet has seeds mixed in, it could be enough for your cardinal to turn into a daredevil. Some individual birds also have a more adventurous streak, and this cardinal may have tried the suet after watching other birds feed that way. It might also be happening because of the time of year, since birds have an instinct to consume more protein during the breeding season.

Q One of our trees has hundreds of holes and sap leaking out of it. An arborist told us it was from a yellow-bellied sapsucker. How can we deter the birds from damaging our trees?

Morrie Hooper YORK, PENNSYLVANIA

Kenn and Kimberly: Sapsuckers pass through your area of Pennsylvania during spring and fall migration, with some staying through the winter. They dig "sap wells," which are small square-like holes about a quarter-inch across, arranged in horizontal rows in bark. These wells continue flowing only so long as the bird keeps them open, and you can stop them by wrapping the affected area with burlap or some other heavy material. But if your tree has hundreds of holes leaking sap, and the holes aren't in horizontal rows, they may be caused by something else, such as insects, bacteria or disease.

A Day In The Life
A sapsucker spends much of its time at its sap wells, licking up sap and insects, drilling holes or chasing off birds that want a sap sample.

Q Do chickadees and goldfinches use nesting houses for shelter during harsh winters?

Mike Chapman
CHISAGO CITY, MINNESOTA

Kenn and Kimberly: There is a link between the kinds of places where birds build nests in summer and the spots they choose for shelter in winter. Birds that nest in tree cavities or birdhouses, such as chickadees, wrens or bluebirds, seek out similar places to sleep at night, especially in cold winter weather. Birds that build nests on open tree branches, such as goldfinches, generally don't go inside birdhouses or other enclosed spots for shelter. On cold winter nights, flocks of goldfinches often sleep sitting close together within the sheltering branches of evergreen trees.

Q I saw a ruby-throated hummingbird trying to get nectar from a dandelion. Is that a normal source for them?

Kris Brown KAUKAUNA, WISCONSIN

Kenn and Kimberly: Like most other hummingbirds, ruby-throats typically seek out long, tube-shaped flowers—they're especially attracted to red ones. Dandelion blooms—flat and yellow—don't fit the usual profile. But ruby-throated hummingbirds have to be more adaptable than many other hummingbirds because they migrate such a long distance through different habitats, dealing with big variations in weather and climate. It's an advantage for them to be flexible and to check out whatever flowers are available. Dandelions do contain some nectar, so it's not necessarily a total waste of effort for the bird.

Q It's been stated that birds have no sense of smell or taste. So why do most species prefer certain seeds?

Betty Robinson
WEST BRANCH, MICHIGAN

Kenn and Kimberly: Birds actually do have some sense of taste. It's not well developed in most species, as evidenced by the use of cayenne pepper in birdseed to discourage squirrels. The question of whether birds can smell needs more study. We do know that some have a highly developed sense of smell. Turkey vultures, for example, have a keen sense of smell, helping them locate the carrion they feed on. It's more likely seed-savvy birds are making selections based on what seeds suit the shape of their bill, and following their instincts for nutritional value and seed quality.

Q Why do cardinals aggressively peck at my vehicle's side mirror?

Patricia Ekakiadis
AVONMORE, PENNSYLVANIA

Kenn and Kimberly: Cardinals, like many other birds, defend a territory during the nesting season to make sure they have enough space and food for themselves, their partner and their young. If a male cardinal sees another male cardinal in his territory, he chases the trespasser away. Unfortunately, he can't tell the difference between a real cardinal and a reflection in a mirror, so he might spend hours trying to chase away a false intruder that can't be intimidated. You might try covering the mirror when you're not driving your car so this defensive cardinal can go about his business.

Q Is this hummingbird taking a nap? It landed on this branch after feeding, leaned back for about a minute and then took off!

Charles Hoysa WARRENTON, VIRGINIA

Kenn and Kimberly: You probably caught your visitor preening or in midstretch. With super long bills and tiny feet, hummingbirds strike pretty odd poses while preening their feathers. Hummingbirds also stretch, just like we do when we get up from the table after a meal. Sometimes they will pause in an odd pose and hold it for up to a minute, for no obvious reason whatsoever.

Q How do you keep woodpeckers from attacking wooden siding?

Robyn Long GREENLAND, NEW HAMPSHIRE

Kenn and Kimberly: Discouraging woodpeckers is a challenge, but there are a few things you can try. Reflective streamers are the most effective, but any item that moves or flutters makes a good deterrent. Create these streamers yourself by cutting a Mylar balloon or aluminum foil into thin strips, taping them to a small dowel rod, and attaching it to the top of any area that you want to protect from the woodpeckers. Keep in mind that if the woodpeckers keep coming back to one spot, the wood may be infested with some kind of wood-boring insects.

Q I watched a red-bellied woodpecker stick its tongue out over and over. What was it doing?

Kimberly Miskiewicz RALEIGH, NORTH CAROLINA

Kenn and Kimberly: Red-bellied woodpeckers use their incredibly long tongues to forage for insects. They stick their tongues into tree cavities and crevices to probe for insects and grubs. The end of their tongue is barbed to allow them to latch on to food. Sometimes they even use them to drink syrupy sugar water from hummingbird feeders. Considering all the places they use their amazing tongues for feeding, they can get messy in a hurry. The bird you watched, sticking its tongue out repeatedly, was probably just cleaning its tongue after foraging.

Who's Who

This is a female red-bellied woodpecker—you can tell because the red mark on the back of its head doesn't extend upward toward the beak.

Did You Know?
Young hummers all look like females when they first leave the nest, so birds with male plumage are a minority by late summer.

Q. Why do only female ruby-throated hummingbirds seem to show up at the feeder on my back porch?

Jamie Viebach NEW LENOX, ILLINOIS

Kenn and Kimberly: Male and female ruby-throats don't ever stay together as pairs. The male has a small territory where he courts any passing female and chases away other males. The female has her own home range, where she raises her young. If a female ruby-throat has her nest nearby, she may come to your feeder regularly; if the neighborhood male's center of activity is farther away, he may be getting his food elsewhere. So in early summer, it's partly a matter of luck.

A black-capped chickadee on a snowy day

Q Where do birds sleep at night, and where do they go during a storm?

Linda Broen MENDOCINO, CALIFORNIA

Kenn and Kimberly: Wild birds are good at finding shelter. Those that raise their young inside holes in trees, such as woodpeckers and bluebirds, often sleep in such cavities at night, at all times of year. Other kinds of birds find protected spots inside dense foliage in trees, shrubs or vines. They may perch close to the trunk on the downwind side. Birds that live out in open fields or shores may simply hunker down where they are, facing into the wind. During stormy weather birds usually go to the kinds of spots where they sleep at night, or make an extra effort to find an even more sheltered place.

Q Why would crows chase an owl? I have seen four or five crows flying after and around a barred owl, cawing and squawking, on several occasions.

Mary Leffler REYNOLDSBURG, OHIO

Kenn and Kimberly: Many kinds of birds will harass owls that they discover in the daytime, in a behavior called "mobbing." Even chickadees will mob little screech-owls. Crows focus on bigger targets like barred owls or great horned owls, and they will also chase hawks and eagles. No one has come up with a complete explanation for why they do this. It may serve to draw attention to these predators so they can't take smaller birds by surprise. In the case of the crows, which are intelligent and curious birds, it may be partly a tough-guy way of having fun!

Q A large flock of vultures roosted in my cottonwood trees last winter. The ground was solid white and the smell was not pleasant. Is roosting a seasonal event? If not, how can I encourage them to roost elsewhere?

Ginger Ferguson WEATHERFORD, TEXAS

Kenn and Kimberly: After a day of working as nature's cleanup crew, vultures gather at night in communal roosts. Unfortunately, once they find a good roosting site, they may return year after year. It's illegal to use lethal methods on vultures, but it may be possible to scare them away. Try disturbing them with loud noises or squirting a water hose when they try to settle in for the evening, and they may seek another site. If they're not so easily discouraged, you might hire a professional animal-control company, but make sure they have a reputation for operating legally and not harming the birds.

Turkey vulture

Barred owls sometimes call and even hunt during the daytime.

Vulture Culture

These raptor look-alikes are typically spotted soaring over open areas, often in small groups known as kettles. Turkey vultures use columns of rising air called thermals to help them effortlessly glide without flapping their wings.

A male northern cardinal attacks his reflection in a window.

Angry Birds

Learn why birds attack windows—and how to make them stop.

By Sally Roth

THWACK! The first smack against the window is awful, making you wonder which bird you'll find lying on the ground outside. Then you hear it again—and again—and again. Upon closer inspection, you see a bird viciously pecking at the window. No, it's not trying to get inside for food. It's actually fighting a furious battle with its own reflection.

During mating season in spring, male birds, and even some females, go into attack mode. At the first glimpse of a trespasser of their own species in the nesting area, they fly into a rage. And when the enemy is a bird's very own reflection—in a window, a patio door, a car mirror or a shiny wheel—the war can go on for weeks.

The enraged bird spends hours in a frenzy. Day after day, he returns to the same place, pecking, clawing, beating with his wings. The attack is distressing and irritating to us, too. The noise, the exhausted bird—we just want it to stop.

Birds that nest close to our houses are the main culprits, with American robins and northern cardinals topping the list. Towhees, bluebirds, mockingbirds, finches, native sparrows and vireos may also see red when they catch a glimpse of their own reflection.

The attacks will often peter out as hormones simmer down after nesting. But robins and cardinals raise more than one brood a season, so they can be hot-tempered for months. And some especially obsessive birds keep up the attacks long after nesting season is done. As soon as an angry bird starts showing its wrath at your window, try to nip the attack in the bud. Otherwise, you may be in for a long battle.

To start with, try pinwheels, balloons, fluttering Mylar strips or a fake owl to shoo the bird away. Another idea: Break up the reflection in the glass by covering it with paper, cloth or netting. But if birds become accustomed to those simple tricks, you might try one of our more offbeat but ingenious tactics listed below.

Winning Strategies

- Enlarge a photo of a human face, print it out and tape it to the inside of the window.
- Lay a brightly colored toy snake on the windowsill, or drape several over a car mirror. Snakes with red and yellow "skin" are best, because this color pattern signals danger to birds.
- Attach a stick-on feeder to the window. Birds often declare a truce near food sources.
- Set up a mirror outside to distract the bird, but keep it out of direct sun to prevent fires from starting.
- Try a Birds-Away Attack Spider. Originally sold to deter woodpeckers, they also scare away window peckers.

MASLOWSKI WILDLIFE

Birds of a Feather Work Together

Don't underestimate the ability of birds to work as a team for survival, nest building and feeding.

By Kenn and Kimberly Kaufman

AVID BIRD-WATCHERS have probably noticed that some birds are solitary, such as the lone hawk perching along the highway. And some are social, such as the goldfinches and cedar waxwings that flock to our gardens. We could say that their degree of social behavior is part of the personality of each species. But when birds gather, it isn't just because they enjoy each other's company. There are practical reasons that explain why some birds flock together and even work together.

Group-Nest Building

For a pair of birds to successfully raise young, building a nest is an important step. Unfortunately for many species, there's no attempt at teamwork: Female robins, cardinals and hummingbirds all build nests with no help from their mates. Even the intricate woven nests of orioles are all the mothers' doing.

But the news about the guys isn't all bad. Some males—including red-eyed vireos, mourning doves, red-tailed hawks, bald eagles and great blue herons—bring building supplies like twigs, grasses and plant fibers for the female to shape into a nest. Among some wrens, the male builds the main structure and the female adds the soft lining.

For one African bird, the sociable weaver, nest building is an important task for an entire flock. A sociable weaver nest may look like a gigantic haystack draped over a short, sturdy tree. But up close, you can see dozens of small entrances on the underside, leading to individual nesting chambers. Sometimes more than a hundred pairs may help to build a single group nest.

Cooperation in the Cafeteria Line

Even a flocking bird, when it comes time to eat, must look out for No. 1. But in some cases, birds will work together to find or catch their food.

In the deserts of the Southwest, a family group of Harris's hawks may hunt together. One or two swoop in to scare a rabbit out of a bush, while

Sociable weavers are communal nesters in Africa. Together they can build an amazing nest (above) that looks like a giant haystack.

another waits to grab it as it dashes away. If their hunt is successful, the hawks will share the meal, with the dominant bird eating first and the others getting the leftovers.

Another fascinating example is the cooperative fishing of American white pelicans. These huge birds will line up side by side on the water and swim together toward the shore, dipping their bills in the water and driving fish ahead of them into the shallows, where they can then be scooped up easily.

Games of Follow the Leader

Here's a wintertime wonder you might see in any neighborhood with plenty of trees: a roving flock of five or six kinds of birds making its way through the woods together. The leaders of the pack will be a flock of chickadees, flitting like acrobats in the outer twigs. Often there will be one or two nuthatches, a downy woodpecker and perhaps a brown creeper following along, clambering up tree trunks. A few titmice, a kinglet or two and sometimes a yellow-rumped warbler may join the flock.

These mixed flocks form because other birds like to follow chickadees around. Chickadees are active, alert birds, always on the lookout in every direction, quick to spot any hawk or other predator that comes near. Birds like nuthatches or creepers, moving along with their faces next to tree bark, may be less likely to notice the approach of danger. But they can simply listen to the chickadees and fly to safety when the usual chatter of the little birds turns to alarm calls.

Ganging Up on the Tough Guys

The concept of safety in numbers gets cranked up another notch when birds engage in mobbing behavior. If songbirds discover an owl roosting in the daytime, they gather around and badger it with alarm calls, sometimes flying at it and even pecking at the back of its head. Small predators like screech-owls are usually mobbed by small songbirds; big ones like great horned owls are more likely to be mobbed by crows or other larger birds. The owls are seldom driven away by this harassment, so it might seem that the mobbing behavior doesn't work. But it does mean that all the birds in the neighborhood know the owl's location, so they won't be taken by surprise.

Child Care by the Flock

If you ever watch a nesting pair of American crows, you might get the impression that more than just two adults are bringing food to the young birds in the nest. And you'd be right. Pairs of crows very often have assistants— usually their own offspring from previous years—bringing food and helping to guard the nest. Some crow nests have five or more helpers in addition to the parents. The same kinds of helpers have been observed in many other species, from purple gallinules to western bluebirds.

Some birds take group nesting behavior to an even higher level. With the groove-billed ani, an odd tropical cuckoo that gets as far north as Texas, up to four pairs of adults cooperate to build one big nest, where all the females lay their eggs.

Acorn woodpeckers work as a group to harvest acorns and store them in holes in trees, to help the flock live through the winter.

All the adults in the group help with incubating the eggs and feeding the young.

The ultimate example of cooperation may be the acorn woodpecker. In western oak woods, these gaudy birds live in colonies of a dozen or more. One, two or three females may lay eggs in a single nest; after the eggs hatch, all the adults in the group feed the young birds. But the woodpeckers don't cooperate just at nesting. They also work as a group every fall to harvest acorns and store them in dead trees riddled with holes, saving up enough food to help the flock live through the winter.

These are just a few examples of the clever ways birds can work together. If you watch carefully, you may discover something new about the birds right outside your window. Even the most common of them can still surprise us.

CHAPTER 2

Migration Journeys & Nesting Habits

From traveling cross-country to building nests for brood after brood, birds sure are busy bodies. Here are some expert insights into our feathered friends' on-the-go lives.

LEFT TO RIGHT: ROBERT MUTCH/SHUTTERSTOCK; WILLIAM LEAMAN/ALAMY STOCK PHOTO; ANNETTE SHAFF/SHUTTERSTOCK

Q There was a flock of red-winged blackbirds at my feeders in January. I usually only see them in the summer months. What's going on?

Irene Peery
CHARLOTTESVILLE, VIRGINIA

Kenn and Kimberly: Red-winged blackbirds have complicated migration patterns. Many of them move to the southern United States for winter, but some large flocks stay as far north as the southern edge of Canada through the whole season. Those wintering flocks wander widely and may go unnoticed until they suddenly arrive en masse at a feeder. Sometime in February or March, at the first hints of spring, the flocks break up as the males go to the marshes (even ones that are still frozen) to start staking out their summer territories.

Q While visiting North Carolina in late spring, I was surprised to spot two male rose-breasted grosbeaks. Is it typical for the birds to be this far south in May?

Chris Hewlett
COLUMBIA, SOUTH CAROLINA

Kenn and Kimberly: That's a lucky sighting. Rose-breasted grosbeaks are common in some places, but mostly farther north in late spring and summer. You're right, that area of southwestern North Carolina would be at the extreme southern edge of their summer breeding range. Since there were two males, it's likely they were migrants, still on their way farther north. On the nesting grounds, they would be quite territorial, and one male would likely chase away any others that got close.

Q One year, a great blue heron that often fished our backyard pond never left to migrate. Is this normal?
Marion Lambert LYNDONVILLE, NEW YORK

Kenn and Kimberly: It's true that most great blue herons migrate to warmer climates in winter, but a few will remain far to the north, especially where some open water gives them access to fish, frogs and other aquatic prey. If the water is temporarily frozen, they may survive by catching mice or other small animals. Staying north is a gamble that doesn't always end well for those lingering.

Q One winter, we had an eastern towhee stop at our feeder with mourning doves and cardinals. Is it common for migrating birds to hang out with nonmigrating birds?

Nancy Jenks TREMPEALEAU, WISCONSIN

Kenn and Kimberly: As you know, eastern towhees usually don't spend the winter as far north as Wisconsin, so this bird was out of place. In this specific situation—when a bird is outside its normal range—it's typical for that bird to join up with other birds that are related or have similar feeding habits. By joining a mixed flock, with more eyes watching for danger, the bird increases its own chance for survival. Since cardinals and mourning doves are seed eaters that often feed on the ground, they were probably the best company that this towhee could find.

Female eastern towhee

Q I've watched American robins building nests. Sometimes they come to the birdbath with dry grass and dip it in the water several times. Why do they do this?

Leona Schroeder FERGUS FALLS, MINNESOTA

Kenn and Kimberly: Mud is an essential part of robin nest architecture. The foundation is constructed of mud that holds the nest together like cement. The mud is typically gathered from a ready source, such as the edge of a puddle or earthworm castings. In drier years, robins have to be more resourceful and manufacture their own. They've been observed carrying dirt in their bills to a birdbath to soak, and splashing in the birdbath before flying to a spot of dust and shaking the water off. There's a good chance that the birds you observed were soaking nest material to make mud.

Down Low
Look for gray catbirds close to the ground. They nest in short shrubs and often hop along the forest floor.

Q I love catbirds, but they seem to leave by mid-July. Where are they going?
Barbara Keefer
MARMORA, NEW JERSEY

Kenn and Kimberly: Catbirds are spring and early summer favorites. But in many places, they become much harder to find by midsummer. They don't start migrating south that early. However, they become much quieter after their young have left the nest and learned to fly, and they often disperse far away from their nesting territories. In late summer, catbirds may move to areas of woodland or dense thickets to look for wild fruits and berries. They spend their time fattening up to prepare for migration, and by the end of summer they may start moving south.

Busy Mom
A female ruby-throat selects a site, builds a nest, incubates eggs and raises young on her own.

Q I recently witnessed a female ruby-throat build a nest and incubate her eggs. Then she abandoned the nest when a male showed up. Why would she do that?

Joseph Salmieri
LINDENWOLD, NEW JERSEY

Kenn and Kimberly: Although it's always guesswork with this kind of situation, we think the timing was probably a coincidence. It's true that a male ruby-throat can be aggressive, but the female is a very tough and tenacious mother dedicated to caring for her nest. In most cases, she wouldn't be driven away by an obnoxious new boy in the neighborhood. It's unfortunate that the female in your yard abandoned her nest, but there was probably some other cause.

Bluebird

Backyard Tip
Get birdhouse dimensions for cavity nesters—such as chickadees, nuthatches, bluebirds and purple martins—on page 252.

Q I never see birdhouse dimensions and entrance hole requirements for birds like goldfinches, mourning doves, pine siskins, purple finches and rose-breasted grosbeaks. Do these birds not use nest boxes?

Beth Patterson
HOUGHTON, MICHIGAN

Kenn and Kimberly: The species most likely to use birdhouses are those that have traditionally nested in holes in trees, either natural cavities or old woodpecker holes. Since they already have the instinct to nest inside such spaces, they readily adapt to an enclosed box with a hole on the side. But most birds don't nest in such places; goldfinches and many other songbirds build open, cup-shaped nests on branches of trees or shrubs. A few birds that nest in the open, such as robins and phoebes, will place their nests on ledges of buildings or on small nest platforms under eaves or on porches. But in general, the only birds attracted to traditional birdhouses are the cavity nesters.

Q I've been trying to attract bluebirds for 10 years, but despite my use of the recommended nest boxes, I never saw one—until late winter of last year, when they started showing up at my feeders! Can you help me understand why? I was assuming they went south for the winter.

Robert Smith COLUMBIA, MISSOURI

Kenn and Kimberly: It's true that most bluebirds vacate the northernmost part of their range in winter. But at your latitude, many small flocks will stay through the coldest months. Ordinarily, they can survive on wild berries and small fruits, but if the weather turns exceptionally harsh, they may wander to new places in search of food, winding up at backyard feeders. If you haven't been able to attract them to nest boxes in spring, you might adjust the locations of the boxes; bluebirds like to be near extensive open areas of short grass. Best of luck attracting them this year!

Q I removed an old bird's nest from a box and a few weeks later a spotted egg appeared. Could this be from an optimistic cowbird?

Charles Hoysa WARRENTON, VIRGINIA

Kenn and Kimberly: This egg, pale with lots of brown dots, could have been laid by a brown-headed cowbird, but other kinds of birds have similar eggs. Cowbirds are brood parasites that always lay their eggs in the nests of other species. But usually the female cowbird carefully chooses an active, occupied nest where the egg is sure to be incubated. It's very unusual for an egg to appear in a vacant nest like this. However, sometimes a female bird is ready to lay an egg and doesn't have a nest available, so she'll just dump it somewhere. That could be what happened here.

Q. A few winters ago, I spotted cedar waxwings eating the fruit off my Cleveland pear trees. Is it normal for them to be here this time of year?

Anna Zimmerman
AVENUE, MARYLAND

Kenn and Kimberly: Cedar waxwings are wanderers, and they may show up anywhere in southern Canada or the lower 48 states, including the coastal plain of Maryland. Classic nomads, they almost always travel in flocks, seeking out trees and shrubs heavy with ripe berries or small fruits. It's normal for them to be in your area, but it's also normal for them to disappear for months at a time. The timing of their travel is very unpredictable, but if you keep an eye on those Cleveland pear trees when the fruits are ripe, you might see waxwings again.

Q. Usually robin nests in my yard have three eggs, but I saw eight one year. Is that normal or are multiple robins using the same nest?

Sommer Raines
CONNERSVILLE, INDIANA

Kenn and Kimberly: When robins find a good site for a nest, they sometimes come back and use it repeatedly, as you've seen. But they typically lay three or four eggs, seldom a clutch of five. When a nest holds six to eight robin eggs, two females probably are laying eggs in the nest—perhaps competing for the site until one gives up. So what you've found is truly unusual, and it's an example of the fascinating discoveries that come with careful observation.

Q. I discovered this newly made nest while prepping my fall garden. What bird nests this late in the year?

Anna Perea LOVELAND, COLORADO

Kenn and Kimberly: You are right, it's an uncommon time of year for nest-building, as well as an unusual location! In your area of Colorado, the builder is most likely a house sparrow. While these enterprising little birds usually place their nests inside holes in trees or structures, they'll sometimes put them in more open places like this spot on your tractor. They also build nests throughout the year. We can't be sure from the photo, but it's possible this nest wasn't made by a bird. It could be the work of some small mammal, maybe a mouse or one of the native wood rats.

Fall Chicks

Attract late-season nesters by planting fall-blooming flowers, native trees and shrubs. It's very important for fledglings to have shelter as they learn to fly. Be sure to keep your birdbath out, too—young birds love to splash around in fresh water!

Q. How many broods do bluebirds have in a year? One pair used my nest box three times last summer.

Francis Coverdale WOODBINE, NEW JERSEY

Kenn and Kimberly: Having bluebirds nest in your yard is a treat—it's great that your property is bluebird-friendly! These beautiful birds begin scouting nest boxes in late February, or earlier in the South. If conditions are favorable, they sometimes nest into August or September. Most pairs raise one or two broods per season, and some raise three. It's rare, but they may have four or five sets of chicks. The number of broods depends on many factors, including weather and food supply. Typically, there are fewer eggs per clutch later in the season.

Q Why do mourning dove pairs build their nests so early in spring?

John Rossino MANAHAWKIN, NEW JERSEY

Kenn and Kimberly: That's a good observation—they do start nesting early in the season. Even in the North they may start their first nest as early as March. In southern states, doves may begin in February or even January. And a pair of mourning doves makes repeated nesting attempts during the year, sometimes raising as many as five broods between March and October. Normally they just lay two eggs per brood. Their nests are made of pine needles, twigs and grass, and are so flimsy that the eggs or young sometimes fall out. So the doves may have an instinct to try over and over to make sure they raise enough young to keep the species going.

Q My shed was left open and I saw an eastern phoebe slip out. Inside was a nest with four white eggs and two speckled eggs. What bird lays eggs and leaves them in another nest?

Patricia Bourgeois
DOUGLAS, MASSACHUSETTS

Kenn and Kimberly: The four white eggs in your photo were laid by the phoebe, but a female brown-headed cowbird is responsible for the two speckled eggs. Cowbirds are brood parasites and never raise their own young. Instead, they lay their eggs in the nests of other songbirds, leaving the unwitting foster parents to hatch the eggs and feed the young. Eastern phoebes build open nests that are easy to find, so they are frequent targets for cowbirds. In some parts of their range, as many as one in four phoebe nests contains cowbird eggs.

Q We were successful attracting ruby-throated hummingbirds with feeders. Will the same group return next year?

Dennis Woods GREENSVILLE, ONTARIO

Kenn and Kimberly: Now that you've had success in attracting the ruby-throats, there's a good chance they'll come back every year. Young hummingbirds usually return to the general area where they were hatched. In addition, hummingbirds have strong spatial memory, and they may return to the same spots where they've found food in the past, even after migrating thousands of miles. If you have sugar-water feeders and flowers ready at the right season, you can expect to have plenty of hummingbirds.

Q. Why do robins sometimes leave the place where they're building a nest and not return for a long time?

Lillie Wrobel DYSART, IOWA

Kenn and Kimberly: There's a lot of variation in how long it takes for the female robin to construct a nest. Rarely, it may take only a couple of days, but usually it's closer to a week, and it can even be up to two weeks, especially in bad weather. Sometimes the female robin stops working on the nest for a few days if there's too much rain. At other times, she may pause for the opposite reason—she needs mud for the nest's foundation and may have to wait for rain if there isn't a muddy spot nearby.

Flying South

Orioles, warblers, tanagers and thrushes are known as neotropical migrants. They breed in Canada and the United States, but flee south to Mexico, Central America, South America or the Caribbean for the winter.

Q. A Baltimore oriole visited our yard in November or December for the past three winters. It ate jelly, cut oranges and seed from a ground feeder. Should that bird have been somewhere else?

Lori Ann O'Shaughnessy
MARLBORO, NEW JERSEY

Kenn and Kimberly: Yes, you're right, most Baltimore orioles migrate to the tropics—or at least to the subtropical edges of the southern United States—for the winter. But during the last couple of decades, increasing numbers have been staying through the winter in the states east of the Appalachians, from Georgia north to New England. The abundance of bird feeders in the region seems to have made the difference. Apparently Baltimore orioles can survive cold winters as long as they find enough food.

Q A vermilion flycatcher visits my desert garden every January. This colorful bird is such a welcome sight! Where is it coming from and traveling to?

Rhonda Rogers TUCSON, ARIZONA

Kenn and Kimberly: Most of the flycatchers in North America are very drab, and most migrate long distances. The stunning vermilion flycatcher is a brilliant exception to both rules. In the Southwest, close to the Mexican border, they can be found all year in some places where trees grow along streams or around ponds. At other places in the same region, these flycatchers migrate short distances, moving to slightly higher elevations in summer. The one that visits your garden is probably not coming from very far away—perhaps from central Arizona, just a little to the north of you.

Q I didn't see a single goldfinch, purple finch or rose-breasted grosbeak at my feeders last spring, but I used to see them all the time. Do birds regularly move to new locations?

Paula Forsythe CAMP DOUGLAS, WISCONSIN

Kenn and Kimberly: Goldfinches and purple finches are famous for their wandering ways. They can be common one year and scarce or completely absent the next. Their numbers may change from month to month, or even from one day to the next. But even if they disappear for a while, there's a good chance they'll come back. Rose-breasted grosbeaks aren't usually so unpredictable, so if they've disappeared from your yard, we wonder if the habitat has changed. Your own yard may look the same, but check the surrounding neighborhood. If there are fewer trees now, it might be less attractive to the grosbeaks.

American goldfinch

Q One day I found two hummingbird nests in my tree. Do they reuse their nests or build new ones?

Kriss Reiff GRAND JUNCTION, COLORADO

Kenn and Kimberly: A hummingbird nest is a tiny marvel. Female hummingbirds use the finest plant fibers and spiderwebs to craft a secure cradle for eggs and young. It's strong for its size, but such a nest is not durable enough for repeated use. Typically, the female will build a new nest for each brood, even within the same year. She may start construction before she finishes feeding the full-grown young from a previous one. In rare cases, a location is so good that females build right on top of the remains of the old nest.

Local Gatherings

Many migrants, such as warblers or kinglets, bypass feeders on their journeys north. To find these spring specialties, head to a wooded area or body of water where the birds are likely to stop and rest before continuing on to their chosen breeding grounds.

Q Help! I've spotted numerous failed bird nests over the years. I don't know if the babies didn't make it, the eggs didn't hatch, or the mother deserted it for some reason. What could be the problem?

Liza Peniston AUGUSTA, KANSAS

Kenn and Kimberly: These distressing nest failures may be caused by several things, including extreme weather. If it's too dry and hot, or raining too much, the parent birds may not find enough food, and they abandon the nests. Prowling predators, such as house cats, raccoons or owls, may take the adults or scare them into leaving, even if the nests are left intact. Or it could be just a coincidence that your local birds have just had bad luck. We hope the situation improves for them!

American robins may have up to three broods in one season.

Q Do birds that have multiple broods in a season reuse the same nest for each?

Liza Peniston AUGUSTA, KANSAS

Kenn and Kimberly: It depends on the species. In general, most multibrooded birds do not reuse the same nest because the materials aren't durable enough to last through more than one brood. There are some exceptions, though. Barn swallows may reuse an old nest, cleaning out some of the debris from the first brood and adding a new layer of mud to the rim. Other songbirds occasionally reuse a nest if it's still in good shape. Large birds like eagles may reuse the same nest, but these species raise only one brood per year.

Did You Know?
When killdeers feel threatened, they feign a broken wing to distract intruders away from the nest.

Q I discovered a killdeer family nesting in the middle of my driveway. I'm worried we'll disturb them or someone else driving in won't see them. Can I relocate the nest to keep it safe?

Margaret Wilcox TRYON, OKLAHOMA

Kenn and Kimberly: Killdeers have an instinct to lay their eggs on hard, open ground, and driveways often fit the profile. Unfortunately, relocating the nest often doesn't work. Ground nesters tend to react strongly to location, and they may not recognize their own eggs if you move them even a few feet away. If you believe they're doomed where they are, you could try moving the eggs to the nearest safe spot and hope that the adults will find them. The good news is that young killdeers can walk shortly after they break out of the shell, so if the eggs make it to hatching, the young will soon be able to scamper to safety.

Q Bluebirds laid three eggs, completely covered the nest and then deserted it. Why would they do this?

Dennis Kibbey NEW VIENNA, OHIO

Kenn and Kimberly: Your bluebirds appear to be victims of a house sparrow invasion. Bluebirds make nests of fine grasses, woven together in a tidy cup. This nest is more loosely formed and messy, and would eventually include scraps of debris, a house sparrow signature. House sparrows are highly competitive, and they often kill cavity nesters like bluebirds. House sparrows are not native or protected by law, so it's legal to remove their nests to protect native birds. If you don't have time to tend the box regularly, it's best to plug the entrance hole until the sparrows lose interest, or take the box down. Better to have no box at all than to allow the sparrows to potentially harm the bluebirds.

Q How can I attract wrens to my backyard to feed and nest?

Barbara Troyer MONROE, INDIANA

Kenn and Kimberly: In Indiana, you're most likely to attract house wrens and Carolina wrens. They're both cavity nesters, so offering a suitable nest box is a good place to start. Place it high enough to be safe from predators, but low enough so you can reach it to clean out in fall. Carolina wrens, in particular, are not picky about nest sites, and may build their nests in hanging flowerpots, mailboxes or even the pockets of jeans on a clothesline. Insects are the staple of wrens' diets, so they rarely come to feeders, although Carolina wrens sometimes eat suet. Wrens are attracted to moving water, so a small waterfall or a dripper might help.

House wren

Migration Secrets Revealed

There's much more to bird migration than meets the eye.

By Ken Keffer

Snow geese migrate north to south, but not all birds follow that same pattern.

Finding Low Ground

Birds like Clark's nutcrackers may travel to lower elevations in winter.
This is known as altitudinal migration.

When large numbers of snowy owls fly south in the winter it's called an irruption.

WHEN WE WERE KIDS we all learned that birds fly south for winter. Even though it was probably one of the first fascinating facts you learned about birds, it's not entirely true.

Bird migration has captivated and confused scientists and birders for hundreds of years. Early naturalists and philosophers often pondered where birds went in the winter. Some theorized that swallows and other species buried themselves in the mud. Others thought that birds wintered on the moon. At one point, the prevailing theory for hummingbirds was that they migrated on the backs of geese. We know now, of course, that none of these are true. We also know that it's an oversimplification to simply state that birds fly south for the winter. Let's explore some of the more interesting migratory fliers and their habits.

Winter Travelers

Migration doesn't just happen in spring and fall. Winter movements of certain species are called irruptions. Unlike traditional migrations that occur every year, irruptions are more sporadic and driven by local conditions. Available food resources for northern birds, like conifer cone crops for finches or lemmings for raptors, can lead to mass movements of birds in search of food.

Snowy owls are likely the poster species for irruptions. It seems individual snowy owls have fan clubs when they arrive anywhere south of the Canadian border. Less noticeable irruption species include purple finches, pine siskins and redpolls. They might get mistaken for house finches or goldfinches as they nibble thistle seed in backyards across the northern tier of states.

Altitudinal Migrants

Migration doesn't have to be a long movement across continents. There are plenty of species that demonstrate altitudinal migration. These birds will move to lower elevations during the harsh winter months. Mountain chickadees can occasionally be seen in towns near the mountains all year, but in the winter, the species moves to lower elevation, visiting feeders in striking numbers. Clark's nutcracker, Steller's jay and even the dark-eyed juncos can also exhibit this seasonal movement instead of traditional migration patterns.

While plenty of mountain species move down the mountain during the winter, the dusky grouse of the Rockies moves uphill. These birds survive the winter by nibbling on conifer needles. Then, as the weather begins to warm and food becomes more available, they will again disperse back to lower elevations.

A Nomad's Life

These nomadic species don't move in a classic, seasonal pattern, but instead, wander throughout the year. It's a highly specialized niche, and there are but a few examples of this behavior. Some populations of red crossbills move far and wide to areas with abundant cone crops. Their unique crossed bills make them dependent on specific food sources and they will move out of areas as food sources deplete. What is especially impressive is that crossbills can adjust the timing of their breeding to take advantage of when abundant resources become available.

The Arctic tern can cover more than 25,000 miles in a single year from the Arctic to Antarctica.

Long-Distance Fliers

While numerous shorebirds and seabirds make epic migration journeys, the Arctic tern arguably wins the gold medal for migration. The Arctic tern follows the summers in both hemispheres. After a short nesting season in the high Arctic, this species heads south—extremely far south. They spend the nonbreeding season near Antarctica. Individuals can cover more than 25,000 miles in a single year. That's about nine trips between New York City and Los Angeles.

Considering its small size, the tiny rufous hummingbird might be the most impressive migrator of all. Rufous hummingbirds have a circular migration route. From their winter ranges in southern Mexico, they work their way up the West Coast. Some will make it as far as southeast Alaska for breeding. Then by July, the males head south. They don't follow the coast back, though. Instead they move from mountain meadow to mountain meadow down the spine of the Rocky Mountains.

Occasionally a rufous hummingbird will drift farther to the east, and a few can be found in the Upper Midwest and beyond each fall.

Ever-Changing Movements

Migration doesn't flip on and off like a light switch. Many factors play a role in the movements of birds. Competition for nest sites and food availability drive migration patterns throughout the year. The length of days helps trigger migration. Weather patterns will often facilitate day-to-day movements. It's easier for birds to fly with the wind than against it. Some birds make epic nonstop journeys, but most take stops along the way, each providing an opportunity to refuel.

For the irruptive finches and raptors of the north, flying south for winter can mean southern Canada and the northern United States. Neotropical migrants breed in North America and winter in Central and South America. Migration is a complex topic with endless nuances. There aren't universal rules that apply to all birds. Even populations of the same species will migrate differently in certain instances. Migration is a fascinating topic and one that gets people excited about birds all year long.

On the Road Again

Red crossbills are considered nomads. They often go where cone crops are most abundant.

Feather Beds

Enter the varied world of nests and discover their real purpose, how they're made, and what they do to shelter precious eggs.

By Ken Keffer

NESTS ARE GENERALLY thought of as a bird's home, but it is more appropriate to consider them a nursery for raising babies. Sarah Winnicki-Smith, a Ph.D. candidate in avian evolutionary ecology at the University of Illinois, Urbana-Champaign, helps clear up other common confusions with nesting. "Adult birds aren't always hanging out at the nest like we might see on television shows," Sarah says.

What types of nests do birds build?

The classic cup of woven sticks is just one type of nest. Shorebird and nightjar nests are barely present, just slight divots on the ground. Orioles construct some of the most elaborate woven baskets, which hang as pendulums from tree branches. A few species, including burrowing owls, puffins and kingfishers, nest in underground tunnels. Primary cavity nesters,

A busy tree swallow gathers nest material.

An Altamira oriole builds its hanging woven nest.

Ground Nesters

Killdeer opt for no-fuss nests by laying eggs in the open, usually on gravel or dirt, before adding sticks, rocks or other natural elements.

Cedar waxwings with nestlings

such as woodpeckers, excavate holes in trees for nesting. Secondary cavity nesters, such as bluebirds and tree swallows, use these holes or artificial nest boxes. "Nests are little climate-controlled structures perfect for eggs and hatchlings," Sarah says.

Who builds the nest?

Nest construction varies across species. Many times, nest building is a collaborative effort. But for some species, such as red-winged blackbirds, the males establish territories and leave the nest construction to the females. For many wrens and other birds, males construct several nests within the territory, and females choose mates based partially on these nests. The females freshen up the chosen nest before laying their eggs.

For most bird species, males and females are ultimately both involved in fledging the young. Sarah says, "To be successful requires a combination of nest construction, sitting on eggs and bringing food resources back."

How are nests constructed?

The architecture of nests is impressive. American dippers build nearly waterproof nests with moss

Robin nest

exteriors along banks of raging streams. Many species add sprigs of certain plants to serve as pest repellents.

During graduate work on grassland birds, Sarah observed meadowlarks weaving grass domes with tunnels facing into the prevailing winds to keep nestlings cool on hot summer days.

Birds also adapt to local conditions. Great horned owls traditionally nest in trees, but they alternatively use ground sites, cliffs, saguaro cactus tops or even buildings. Notoriously, owls often take over old nests of hawks, crows, herons or even squirrels.

When do birds lay eggs?

It's an oversimplification to think that birds nest only in summer. In the southern reaches of the United States, breeding can happen during any month. Even in the North, raptor courtship may start by late fall, and female owls, hawks and eagles may be sitting on eggs by February. American goldfinches are famously late-season nesters. Their breeding cycle matches up with crops of native thistles. This linkage with weather and food is what drives the timing of nesting, which can happen as late as September.

"In the Midwest, American robins start building nests when it is still cold, but warmer temperatures and food resources are available when the young hatch," Sarah says.

How long does it take for eggs to hatch?

There are generally two approaches to egg laying and they affect the time an egg takes to hatch. Altricial species (such as songbirds) are born nearly featherless. These helpless hatchlings depend on adults for warmth and food for weeks before fledging. Precocial species (such as shorebirds, waterfowl and grouse) lay larger eggs and have longer incubation periods. Even though the eggs may have been laid days apart, they hatch at the same time, and all the hatchlings hit the ground running.

Do birds reuse nests?

Some large birds, such as eagles or herons, may use the same nest for years, but most kinds opt for new sites every time. A lot of factors go into whether individual birds will lay eggs more than once per year. "Many species can renest if attempts fail early in the breeding season,

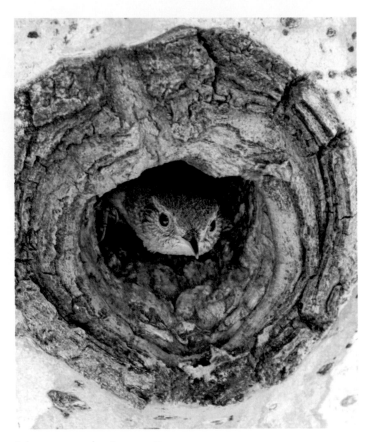

A house wren peeks out of a nest hole in an aspen tree.

and some regularly produce multiple broods annually," Sarah says. Birds most often pick a different location for later nesting sites, even after successful attempts. One grasshopper sparrow that Sarah monitored moved more than 3 miles between nests.

For the most part, songbirds abandon their nests after the breeding season. A few, especially cavity nesters, might return to roosting sites, but they don't generally use the same hollows as they did before.

Do some species lay eggs in the nests of others?

Around 1% of birds don't build a nest of their own. Instead, these brood parasites lay eggs in the nests of other species. Brown-headed cowbird eggs have been documented in the nests of more than 200 other types of birds.

"It's really amazing that these baby birds can grow up in such different environments," says Sarah.

Roof Over Their Head

Phoebes look for overhangs when choosing a nesting location, often selecting barns and other human-made structures.

CHAPTER 3
Identify Birds

Readers share encounters with mysterious feathered visitors, while our experts provide tips for proper identification and advice on how to differentiate juvenile birds from adults.

Q I noticed this bird perched on our fence. Can you identify it?

Steve Martin OMAHA, NEBRASKA

Kenn and Kimberly: This bird is usually seen in flight, so it can be genuinely confusing when we find one perched. It's a common nighthawk. Notice the tiny bill, which opens up to reveal a huge, gaping mouth for catching insects in flight. Other ID points include a big head, short neck and very long wings that extend from the shoulder to the end of the tail. Mottled brown feathers make good camouflage when the nighthawk is at rest on the ground or a tree branch. The odd perching position of this bird, plopped down on the fence, is because nighthawks have very small feet.

Q What's this yellow bird that visits my backyard feeder?

Christine Ramey
SPRINGFIELD, GEORGIA

Kenn and Kimberly: Lucky you! That's a very special visitor because it's a member of the warbler family. And since warblers are insect eaters, most aren't attracted to feeders. The main exception is the pine warbler, which is the bird in your photo. They regularly visit suet feeders, especially in the southern states during winter. This particular warbler is a male. Key field marks to note include the bright yellow underparts with streaks at the sides of the chest, and the detailed pattern around and below the eyes.

Q What kind of bird is this? I saw it in a swampy area in my home state.

Gail Jakubiak HUDSON, FLORIDA

Kenn and Kimberly: Mainly a winter visitor in Florida, this yellow-rumped warbler arrives in late fall and leaves in early spring. In this pose, most of its key field marks are hidden, including a yellow patch at each side of the chest and its trademark yellow rump patch. But it's recognizable by the contrast of its brown cheek patch, white throat and striped chest. While many warblers leave the U.S. to fly deep into the tropics in winter, yellow-rumped warblers can thrive in cold weather by eating nutrition-dense berries.

Q We spotted this bird in our backyard. What is it?

Julia Worth WEYMOUTH, MASSACHUSETTS

Kenn and Kimberly: Some birds that show up in summer can be genuinely confusing because they are very young, having just learned to fly, and look noticeably different from adults. This one is a good example: It's a young eastern phoebe. It probably left the nest and became independent from its parents just a few days before you saw it. Where the adult phoebe has a white throat and rather plain wings, this youngster is a dingy brown on the throat and chest and has pale cinnamon-buff wing bars. By early fall, with some of these feathers replaced, it will look more like its parents.

Q Can you identify this tiny bird?

Dave Johnson COLGATE, WISCONSIN

Kenn and Kimberly: The drab little ruby-crowned kinglet can be confusing. It's called "ruby-crowned" because the male has red feathers on the top of his head, but these are usually hidden. Better field marks include its tiny size, short-tailed shape, thin bill, whitish ring around the eye and double white and black bar across each wing. Kinglets are so active that it's hard to get a good look, so we're impressed that you got such a fine photo! But you can often recognize them by their typical action of rapidly flicking their wings open and shut when they pause on a perch.

Did You Know?

Ruby-crowned kinglets can have as many as 10 to 12 eggs in a single clutch.

Q Do male American goldfinches lose their black caps in winter?

Kitty Carty PRINEVILLE, OREGON

Kenn and Kimberly: Goldfinches, like most small birds, molt all their feathers at the end of summer or during fall. By the time winter arrives, the snappy yellow and black plumage of the males is replaced by a new, but much more drab, set of feathers, lacking the black cap and most of the gold tones. This molt during the fall is far less noticeable than the transition back to their bright breeding plumage in spring. It's fascinating to watch how quickly the males transition back into their dapper summer plumage.

Q Four of these birds showed up in our yard. What are they?

Patsy & Steve LaFlam
PLATTSBURGH, NEW YORK

Kenn and Kimberly: What you saw was undoubtedly a family group: one adult green heron and three of its young. It's definitely an unusual sight for most backyards. Green herons are among the smallest members of the heron family, only about the size of a crow. Typically they build their nests in trees or shrubs at water's edge, but sometimes they choose a site in a tree some distance away.

Q Can you identify this handsome hawk?

Max Van Orsdel ROCKLIN, CALIFORNIA

Kenn and Kimberly: The slim shape and long tail are typical of an accipiter hawk; the blue-gray back and reddish chest indicate an adult Cooper's hawk or sharp-shinned hawk. Those two are very similar, but several things on this bird point to a Cooper's hawk. Its head has a squarish look, coming to a corner at the back of the crown, and the top of the head is very black. A sharp-shinned hawk's head would look more rounded and its crown would be more evenly blue-gray. This hawk also has the thicker legs of a Cooper's, while the legs of a sharp-shinned would look pencil thin.

Q Is this new guest a house finch or a purple finch?

Jim Gordon DASSEL, MINNESOTA

Kenn and Kimberly: Telling house and purple finches apart is a common backyard challenge over much of North America. On the males, one of the first things to look for is the distinct pattern on the sides of the body, below the wings. House finch males have dark stripes there (as seen in your photo), while purple finches don't. A female house finch has a fairly plain brown face, while a female purple finch has a contrasting white eyebrow and whisker mark. House finches also have a smaller beak, a slimmer body, shorter wingtips and a longer tail than the purple finch.

Winter Clothes

Many birds, like American goldfinches and yellow-rumped warblers, stick around parts of the U.S. all winter. They're just more difficult to spot because they molt into more subdued tones for the cold months, only sporting dull patches of yellow.

Q What kind of bird is this?

Brian Herrmann PARMA, OHIO

Kenn and Kimberly: This shy bird hiding among the branches is a fox sparrow—among the largest and most beautiful of our native sparrows in North America. They spend the winter mostly in the southern states and go far north into Canada for the summer nesting season. The key to identifying the one in your photo is the mix of gray and foxy reddish brown, which is especially bright on the tail.

Q I found this nest about a foot off the ground in an elm sapling in a grassy area. What kind of bird built it?

Cris Nichols MAYETTA, KANSAS

Kenn and Kimberly: It's a challenge to identify nests. Many kinds of birds build similar ones, and appearances vary depending on the materials available. And eggs are only a little more distinctive than nests. From the photo, we can't be sure of the size of the nest and egg. If they were small, this may be the nest of a chipping sparrow. The egg has the right color and pattern, and the nest shows a coarse outer layer and a lining of very fine materials. Chipping sparrows will use soft horsehair for nest lining if they can find it.

Q Can you please identify this tanager?

Debbie McKenzie
ANNISTON, ALABAMA

Kenn and Kimberly: You've captured this tanager in an intriguing stage of molt. The gray-brown streaks are the remains of juvenile plumage, just being replaced by the yellow feathers of its first-year immature plumage. Juvenile tanagers aren't even illustrated in most bird guide books, because they wear this plumage for such a brief time. At this stage, summer and scarlet tanagers can look very similar. Its bill may not be fully grown yet, but already looks too large for a scarlet tanager. The wings don't look dark enough either. So it's a very young summer tanager, and it probably hatched not far from your yard.

Q I took this photo near Scottsdale, Arizona. I think it's a young male, but is it an Anna's or a black-chinned hummer?

Steve Dummermuth Jr.
CEDAR RAPIDS, IOWA

Kenn and Kimberly: Immature male hummingbirds are tricky to identify, because they're often somewhere between the appearance of a female and an adult male. We think this is a young male Costa's hummingbird for several reasons. The dark outline of the throat patch, extending down and back below the eye, is very typical of Costa's at this stage, and so is the patch of pinkish purple on the lower throat. Also, the breast and sides are clear whitish—most Anna's and black-chinneds tend to show more of a gray-green wash on the sides.

Q Do Anna's hummingbirds normally have white-tipped tails?

Kathy Hitzemann
FREELAND, WASHINGTON

Kenn and Kimberly: For most of the North American species of hummingbirds, including Anna's, the females and young birds have big white spots on the tips of their outer tail feathers, while the adult males don't. When the birds are perched, those white spots are often hidden by dark central tail feathers, so it's easy to overlook the white patches unless you get a close look while the birds are hovering and fanning their tails. When the birds are perched, sometimes the tail feathers are disarranged so the white spots are revealed.

Q What kind of sparrow is this?

Urszula Stepniak ADA, MICHIGAN

Kenn and Kimberly: The bird is a song sparrow, and we would guess that the photo was taken sometime in summer. These sparrows molt into a fresh plumage in fall, with brand-new feathers, so their markings are sharper from fall to early spring. By summer, after the adult birds have worked hard to raise their young, the feathers look more worn and frayed, and the browns may have faded to a more reddish color. But this bird still shows typical markings, including the face pattern with its bold "whisker mark" at the edge of the throat.

Q This yellow-shafted flicker has a faint mustache. Is it a young male or female?

Rebecca Granger BANCROFT, MICHIGAN

Kenn and Kimberly: That's a wonderful close-up photo, displaying lots of feather detail. The bird appears to be female, although it shows more contrast in the mustache area than usual. Juvenile male northern flickers (both yellow- and red-shafted forms) have a very pale orange mustache at first, which is replaced with the classic black or red mustache that adults sport before midautumn. So in late summer or early fall, we might see young male flickers with patchy mustache marks, but a bird with this subtle pattern is much more likely to be female.

Good Fats

Many winter birds, including northern flickers, chickadees and nuthatches, appreciate suet for its high fat content. Peanut butter and pure lard are also healthy substitutes. Avoid using bacon grease—some of the additives are harmful for birds.

Q What's the best way to differentiate between robin and downy woodpecker calls?

Kayla Bezkorow BRANTFORD, ONTARIO

Kenn and Kimberly: The sharp alarm note of an American robin does sound similar to the single peep of a downy woodpecker. To our ears, the robin's note is much sharper and ends with a piercing *eenk*; while the downy is a somewhat less emphatic *peep*. Identifying birds by their voices is a wonderful skill, but can be tricky. It requires a good deal of time and patience. The good news is that the best way to study birdsong is to spend more time outside with the birds. Not a bad homework assignment!

Little Jewel
Costa's, like this male, weigh in at only one-tenth of an ounce. Their crouched posture makes them look even smaller.

Q. Two kinds of hummingbirds visit our yard: black-chinneds and Costa's. One is a young male Costa's whose throat patch is just beginning to show, and I always wonder how old he is. What is the life span of a hummingbird?

Terry Burkhart LANDERS, CALIFORNIA

Kenn and Kimberly: Unfortunately these tiny creatures don't live very long. Based on banding studies, 7 or 8 years is a ripe old age for most hummingbirds in the wild. Ruby-throated hummingbirds have lived 9 years, and one banded female broad-tailed hummingbird in Colorado made it to 12. A zoo that's properly set up to care for these birds may help to stretch longevity. For example, two resident black-chinned hummingbirds at the Arizona-Sonora Desert Museum in Tucson lived to 13 or 14 years old. We don't have much information on the Costa's hummingbird, but a male with his gorget (throat patch) just developing would be a little less than 1 year old.

Q. If young owls are called owlets and young eagles are called eaglets, what do you call young hawks, such as this Cooper's? Hawklets?

Linn Fairchild LA HABRA, CALIFORNIA

Kenn and Kimberly: Hawklet is a fun word, but it probably won't catch on as a general term for young hawks. We're not aware of any standard word for these young birds; we usually call them nestlings while they're still in the nest and fledglings after they learn to fly, as with most other young birds. We usually avoid using the word "owlet" for young owls, because there are actual species of small owls that are called owlets. For example, the spotted owlet of southern Asia is completely different from the spotted owl of western North America.

Q These birds greeted us at our feeders in spring. We think they are juvenile red-headed woodpeckers. Is that assumption correct?

Robert Tripp EFFINGHAM, ILLINOIS

Kenn and Kimberly: Yes, you've got it. This can be a tricky ID, too. Since adult red-headed woodpeckers wear a simple design of solid black, white and red, it's surprising to see all the intricate markings of brown on the juveniles. That brown pattern probably makes good camouflage, especially when they're sitting against tree trunks, still learning to watch for danger. Juvenile red-headed woodpeckers don't develop red on the head until sometime in their first fall or winter, and they may not have complete adult plumage until they are more than a year old.

Q I saw this bird at Virginia Beach, but I can't seem to identify it. Can you help me?

Andrea Valle VIRGINIA BEACH, VIRGINIA

Kenn and Kimberly: It's a boat-tailed grackle (a regular along the Virginia coast), but more specifically, it is a young male molting into adult plumage. The head and parts of the bird's wing still have brown juvenile feathers, but the black adult feathers have grown in on other areas of the wing and body. The tail feathers are frayed, but after the new feathers grow in, the tail will look longer and blacker. The bird may be in an awkward adolescent phase now, but it certainly won't stay that way for long.

Q I photographed this migrating warbler. What species is it?

Bill Klipp KEY WEST, FLORIDA

Kenn and Kimberly: That's a fine photo capturing a very interesting behavior! You're right in calling this a warbler; it's a palm warbler in winter plumage. Key field marks include the strong face pattern, with dark eyeline and pale eyebrow, and the touch of yellow under the base of the tail. Palm warblers spend the summer mostly in spruce bogs of eastern Canada and migrate toward the Caribbean in fall, spending the winter on islands, along coasts, and in parts of the Southeast, including Florida. Insects make up most of their diet, but they also go for natural nectar sources, as this little one is demonstrating.

Q Is this a juvenile sparrow? I was very surprised to see yellow on its body.

Rosella Brzozowski CRYSTAL LAKE, ILLINOIS

Kenn and Kimberly: The bird does suggest a sparrow, aside from all that yellow, but it's actually a juvenile bobolink. In spring and summer, the adult male displays a sharp pattern of black, white and yellow, but females, juveniles and winter males all resemble sparrows. Bobolinks, which nest in prairies, meadows and hayfields, have showed declining numbers in recent years, so we're glad that they're nesting in your area. They're long-distance fliers, migrating all the way to South America for the winter.

Q I came across this oriole look-alike. What bird is it?

Kelly Schmitz CHILTON, WISCONSIN

Kenn and Kimberly: You're right to tag it as an oriole: It's a young male orchard oriole. In their first year, male orchard orioles look like females, sporting yellow-green feathers. Sometime that fall, they develop a black mask and they'll look like the bird in your photo for the next 12 months. In the fall of their second year, they molt their feathers again, finally donning their rich chestnut and black mature feathers. Orchard orioles used to be rare in Wisconsin, but in recent years they have been extending their range northward, so you may start to see them more often.

Q I heard the sound of wings flapping in my backyard, and a very large pair of birds flew a lap above my house before landing in the oak trees in back. What kind of birds were they?

Ashley Crato PORT ORANGE, FLORIDA

Kenn and Kimberly: Congratulations! These are yellow-crowned night-herons. For most of the year, these birds are not conspicuous; they spend the day roosting in dense trees, coming out at dusk to hunt for crabs and small fish along the edge of the water. But in breeding season they become much more active. During courtship they will fly around together in the daytime; they'll even perform displays that involve fanning their wings and spreading all their plumes. Yellow-crowned night-herons will sometimes raise their young in suburban neighborhoods or even city parks if there are tall, dense trees where they can build their nests.

Q My dogs alerted me to this bird peering in our windows. What kind of hawk is it?

Hank Mendenhall
PUNTA GORDA, FLORIDA

Kenn and Kimberly: This looks like a young Cooper's hawk. Adults are blue-gray above and pale reddish on the chest, but for about their first year of life, the young birds are brown, with dark stripes on a white chest. (Young sharp-shinned hawks are similar to young Cooper's, but their dark stripes below tend to be wider, more blurry and more reddish brown.) Cooper's hawks are curious, alert birds that often visit cities and towns, where they investigate yards and often perch close to houses.

Q We live in the north Georgia mountains. This bird has been visiting our finch food feeder for a few days. Can you tell us what it is?

Tracy Langford BLUE RIDGE, GEORGIA

Kenn and Kimberly: That's a great sighting! The bird is a male blue grosbeak. It's a fairly common summer resident in the southern and central U.S., but it spends most of its time in dense thickets and woodland edges, so it's often hard to see. It's not a common visitor to bird feeders. The blue grosbeak is related to the indigo bunting, but it's bigger, with rich chestnut-brown markings on the wings and a much larger bill. Incidentally, that's a beautiful feeder; no wonder the birds like it!

Q Some cedar waxwings lack their namesake waxy red wingtips. Can this be explained by age or gender?
Bill Heban ROSSFORD, OHIO

Kenn and Kimberly: That's a good observation. Waxwings are named for the waxy red tips on certain wing feathers, but individuals vary in how many red tips they have. In general, males have more than females, and adults have more than young birds. An adult male cedar waxwing may have six to eight red tips, while adult females usually have five to seven. Young females often have fewer than five, and sometimes none at all. Males and females are almost identical otherwise, though the throat is more solidly black on males. This bird, with its dark gray throat and no red on the wing, is almost certainly a female less than a year old.

Seeing Orange
If you spot a cedar waxwing with an orange tail tip instead of a traditional yellow one, it may have overindulged on the berries produced by a variety of honeysuckle.

Q Spring weather here includes 90-degree temperatures, so birds regularly cool off in our baths. What birds did I capture here at my backyard birdbath?
Sylvia Hiltz CARRIZO SPRINGS, TEXAS

Kenn and Kimberly: The two birds enjoying your birdbath are female orioles. They're probably orchard orioles, although the female hooded oriole looks similar—it's challenging to tell these two apart without a good look at the bill. Actually, your area of southwestern Texas is the best place in the U.S. to see a variety of orioles, with six different kinds possible during the year. Hooded orioles and Bullock's orioles are summer residents, orchard orioles are common migrants that may stay through the summer, Audubon's orioles are uncommon there all year, and Scott's orioles and Baltimore orioles stop through during migration seasons. Keep a close watch; any of these orioles might show up at your refreshing birdbath!

Did You Know?
Vireos are known for their songs. They sing short phrases in a robin-like tone.

Q I've searched my field guide and cannot identify this bird and the unique nest I spotted from my back deck. Can you help me identify it?

Janet Holdmann BUTLER, WISCONSIN

Kenn and Kimberly: That's a fine bird and nest to see from your back deck! It's a red-eyed vireo, but it might be hard to find in the book because the effects of lighting are changing its appearance in this photo. A lot of light is being reflected onto the bird from the surrounding leaves, making it seem far more yellowish than it really is. We're identifying it by the shape of the bill and pattern of the face. The nest structure is typical, too. A vireo nest is shaped like a little pouch, suspended from twigs by its edges.

Take a look at how small the downy on the left is compared to the hairy woodpecker on the right.

Identifying Downy and Hairy Woodpeckers

Figure out which woodpecker is which with these expert tips.

By Kenn and Kimberly Kaufman

DOWNY WOODPECKERS are among our most common and beloved backyard birds, but did you know they have a look-alike cousin: the hairy woodpecker? Telling downies apart from hairy woodpeckers can be a challenge, but once you know what to look for, it's not so tough after all!

Look at the plumage

Smartly patterned in black and white, with a touch of red on the males, downy woodpeckers and hairy woodpeckers look remarkably similar to each other. Both downies and hairies have black central tail feathers and white outer tail feathers, but there are a few sneaky clues to differentiate between the two. Downy woodpeckers have a few black bars or spots on their white outer tail feathers, while the outer tail feathers on the hairy are usually plain and unmarked.

Size them up

The hairy woodpecker is distinctly larger than its downy cousin—about 9 inches from the tip of its bill to the end of its tail. (To compare, the downy woodpecker is about 6½ inches long.) Their size difference is surprisingly hard to see, except when they're side by side, which doesn't happen often. A more reliable way to notice their size differences is to look at the shape of their bills. The downy has a tiny, stubby beak, barely as long as the distance from the front of its head to its eye. The hairy woodpecker's bill is much longer and stronger, nearly as long as the bird's head.

Listen carefully

A downy woodpecker's call is a short, friendly *pik* and a high-pitched, descending whinny. The hairy woodpecker has a more attention-grabbing call: a sharp, arresting *peek*!, like the sound of a squeaky dog toy. Hairies also have a sharp rattle that stays at one pitch, unlike the downy woodpecker's call.

Observe habitat preferences

Although downy and hairy woodpeckers share some of the same habitats, downy woodpeckers are more likely to be seen in suburbs and small parks. Hairy woodpeckers generally prefer heavily forested areas with large trees.

Be wary of identical fledglings

It's easy to confuse young downy and hairy woodpeckers. While both woodpecker adult males have a red patch on the back of the head, fledglings just leaving the nest have red on top. Sometimes on young hairy woodpeckers, the patch is yellow, not red. Youngsters may have black marks on their sides or white back stripes.

Attracting Woodpeckers

- Serve suet and suet cakes in wire mesh baskets hanging on trees or in holes drilled into logs.
- Offer peanuts and sunflower seeds in any kind of feeder that allows a place for tree-climbing birds to cling.
- Leave dead trees standing, as long as they don't pose a safety hazard. Woodpeckers (and many other cavity-nesting birds) will reward you with a visit.

Identifying Mystery Birds

Use these techniques when a puzzling bird flies past.

By Kenn and Kimberly Kaufman

EVEN IF YOU KNOW your local birds, sometimes an unfamiliar one will appear that doesn't match anything you've seen before. Here are some pointers and questions to consider the next time you spot a baffling bird.

Take it all in

Don't immediately reach for your field guide. Instead, pay attention to the bird. What does it look and sound like? How does it move? The book won't fly away, but the bird will.

Compare size and shape

A bird's size can be hard to judge, so compare it to a well-known species. It's more helpful to say "robin-size" or "smaller than a sparrow" than estimate its size in inches. Notice its body and bill shape, too. Is the bird stout or slender? Long-tailed or short-tailed? Is the bill thin like a warbler's or thick like a finch's?

Consider surroundings

An open field is home to different birds than a forest or the open waters of a lake. Even within the same habitat, different birds may seek out a range of niches. Is your mystery bird hopping on the ground, climbing up a tree trunk or flitting around the twig tips? These behaviors offer clues.

Look for field marks

The markings on a bird can tell you a lot. Does it have a ring around its eye or a stripe above it? Is the chest spotted or striped?

Watch out for tricky birds

Some physical oddities can be chalked up to perplexing plumage of common local species.

Eastern bluebird with juvenile

Is it possible the bird is leucistic with patches of unusual white feathers? Could it be stained from something it was eating? Could it be a young bird with juvenile plumage that is different from that of its parents?

Write down details

Don't rely on memory alone. It's best practice to record your observations before you look in a book or online to identify the bird. If you start writing a description while the bird is still around, you may notice details you would otherwise miss.

Take a photo

Even a distant image may help pin down the ID. If your phone has a camera, take advantage and snap several pictures. Just don't waste a lot of time trying to get the perfect shot; you need to look at the bird, too.

Did You Know?

You can easily identify a wood thrush by common field marks,
such as a white eye ring and spotted chest.

CHAPTER 4

Gardening Guidance

Want a garden that makes the neighbors green with envy? From seed starting to proper maintenance and common plant problems, care for your backyard beauties with this advice.

Q I tried my luck at growing radishes in a pot. They sprouted beautifully and had five leaves, but then nothing happened. What's going on?

Elizabeth Barnhart BAKERSFIELD, CALIFORNIA

Melinda: All leaves and no roots is a common complaint from gardeners who grow radishes. Well-draining soil, thinning and proper fertilization are key to growing full-size roots on radishes. Avoid high-nitrogen fertilizers that encourage top growth and discourage root development.

Thin the seedlings to about 1 inch apart once they develop two true leaves. This creates room for the roots to reach full size. Use the removed leaves as greens for salads, sandwiches and snacks.

If you're still having trouble, test the soil to see if it needs phosphorus, which encourages root growth.

Q Short-lived red and orange blooms appear on this hibiscus. Are two different kinds of plants in this pot?

James Taylor Sr. LEWISBURG, PENNSYLVANIA

Melinda: Take a close look at the base of the plant for your answer. Two different hibiscus plants are sometimes put together in one pot, often braided together for a creative display. But if the orange and red blooms appear on different branches that arise from the same trunk, then a mutation on a single plant must have occurred. The mutation would cause the change in flower color on one branch, creating this multihued display.

Q I keep a shamrock plant in an east-facing window. I try my best to keep it healthy, but the leaves have shriveled twice. I remove the dead material and it grows back. What's happening?

Jackie Hildebrand
STRONGSVILLE, OHIO

Melinda: Shamrock plants (*Oxalis*), which are actually members of the wood sorrel family, normally go dormant for short periods. The leaves naturally start to yellow and dry. When this occurs, water less often until the leaves are completely brown. Then place the plant in a cool, dark location until new growth begins. Move it back into bright light as soon as any green appears, and start watering it often enough to keep the soil slightly moist. Enjoy the show as new growth shoots up.

Grow Outdoors
Sunflowers are tricky to transplant when started indoors. It may be easiest for gardeners to wait until the last frost passes and then plant outside.

Q Do you have any tips for planting sunflowers early in the season?
Joy Chanin MARIETTA, GEORGIA

Melinda: Consider covering young seedlings to protect them from birds, small mammals and cooler soil temperatures in early spring. Place lightweight floating row covers over new plantings. These fabrics allow air, light and water through, but trap heat around the plants. This speeds seed germination and helps protect young seedlings from unexpected cold weather. The covering also keeps out birds and discourages other animals that may try to snack on your sunflowers.

Q. Should basket mums be cut back to the ground after blooming, or pulled and replanted next fall?

Margie Sloane OVIEDO, FLORIDA

Melinda: Growing mums in Florida poses different challenges and opportunities than growing them in northern states. Cut them back to where the foliage is fullest after the flowers fade. New green shoots will appear and you may eventually be rewarded with another smaller flush of flowers. Depending on the weather, you may have sporadic flowering into spring. Those in South Florida find it best to treat them like annuals, and you may, too.

Q. Can my cat be harmed if it eats the herbs I grow on the windowsill?

Susanne Ketner MIDDLETOWN, VIRGINIA

Melinda: When checking a plant's toxicity to pets, I always consult *aspca.org*, the American Society for the Prevention of Cruelty to Animals website, which has a fairly comprehensive list of toxic and nontoxic plants. The University of North Carolina Extension Gardener Plant Toolbox at *plants.ces.ncsu.edu* is another good resource. It provides images along with detailed plant care and safety information. Here are a few herbs to grow and some to keep away. Safe : basil, cilantro, lemon balm, rosemary and sage. Poisonous: Common mint, lavender, lemon grass, oregano and parsley.

Q Besides mums, what should I plant to get more flowers and color in autumn?

Judy Roberts GRAYTOWN, OHIO

Melinda: Mums definitely signal the end of the growing season, but native asters, turtleheads and goldenrods are also excellent options. Try sunny Ohio goldenrod or the cultivar Fireworks (shown here). They provide nectar for pollinators preparing for winter or migrating to their southern homes. One of my favorite nonnative plants is toad lily. The flowers remind me of orchids and appear along or at the tip of the plant's stem. Native and noninvasive ornamental grasses also provide texture year-round, and many flower in fall, producing attractive seed heads that last through winter.

Q How do I reduce stress on my plants when moving them inside the house?

Susan Zarecky HAYES, VIRGINIA

Melinda: Gradually introduce plants to their new home to reduce stress. Start by moving them to the sunniest window in your home. If possible, quarantine them from other plants and watch them for a few weeks to make sure they aren't carrying insects. Little by little, move the plants to spots with lower light until they reach their winter location. Consider supplementing natural light with artificial light, which is especially helpful in homes with fewer large windows. Adjust your watering schedule to accommodate for less light and higher humidity. Increase humidity by placing your plants closer together or on trays with pebbles and water. Then be sure to wait until spring to fertilize.

Q Do I need to trim my perennials once the frost kills them?

Joanne Tanner HAMBURG, NEW YORK

Melinda: Let healthy perennials, including grasses, stand for winter. This increases hardiness as the plants provide added insulation for the roots by catching more snow, nature's winter mulch. Standing plants provide motion and texture, and seedheads attract and feed the birds that add color to an often drab winter landscape. Many beneficial insects overwinter in the stems and under the plants in the leaf litter, too. Wait as late as possible in spring to remove the top growth and then go ahead and compost.

Butterfly Favorite
Sedum bursts to life in late summer. Its bloom clusters persist into fall and attract many butterfly species, like this red admiral.

Q Every year my sedum start out OK, but by blooming time they are flat on the ground. I hear I should cut them back, but when and how far do I go?

Bill Spain BELLEVUE, NEBRASKA

Melinda: Grow sedum in full sun and well-draining soil for best results. Plants tend to flop when they're in too much shade or moist rich soils that can also stunt their growth. Pruning helps prevent flopping when you grow sedum in less-than-ideal conditions. Cut the plants back halfway when they reach 8 inches tall. Pruned plants do produce plenty of flowers. They may be a bit smaller, but the overall floral display is about the same.

Q When should I split my peonies: in the fall or spring?

Michael Picard GREEN BAY, WISCONSIN

Melinda: Peonies are long-lived and need dividing only when you want to move them or start new plants. For best results, dig and divide peonies in fall after the leaves turn yellow or are killed by frost. Carefully remove the clump and cut it so each section has at least three to five eyes. Plant the rhizome (the swollen underground stem) in properly prepared soil, with the eyes no more than 1 to 2 inches deep, and water thoroughly. It's normal for plants to not bloom the following spring; it may take them a year to establish and start flowering.

Q Some daffodil plants in my garden did not bloom. Is there any hope that they'll have flowers this coming spring? I do leave the greens until they turn brown.

Mary Anne Christoffersen
STATEN ISLAND, NEW YORK

Melinda: Frost, excess shade and overcrowding may prevent daffodils from flowering. Buds of early-blooming daffodils are often killed by late spring frosts. Since the flower buds look similar to a leaf tip when they first expand, the frost damage is often overlooked. In that case, you should have spring blooms if the weather cooperates.

If frost was not an issue, evaluate the amount of sunlight your plants are receiving. Maturing trees, new structures and additional plantings can increase shade to the point where the plants won't bloom. Crowding causes a reduction in flowering. Dig and divide overcrowded plants, and move those that are in heavy shade if that's the problem. Do this as the foliage declines or in fall when you would normally plant new bulbs.

Q Every year I get rushed and careless and lose a few large pots to cracking or chipping. How should I care for my pots if I leave them outdoors?

Joan Oswald APPLE VALLEY, MINNESOTA

Melinda: Fall cleanup is a busy time, and it is easy to rush and miss some tasks. When soil freezes it expands and may cause your pots to crack. To avoid this, empty the soil and overturn your glazed and clay pots. Cover the overturned pots with a large garbage bag to prevent unglazed pots from absorbing water and cracking when the water freezes and expands.

Terra-Cotta Conundrum
The classic garden pots crack when exposed to damp winter weather because they're made of clay, which soaks up moisture.

Q I planted hibiscus in two colors: solid burgundy and white with a burgundy center. Years later, some are the original colors, but others are bubblegum pink to dark red. Why?

Lorraine Tighe LA PORTE, INDIANA

Melinda: One or more things could be creating this kaleidoscope of colors. Mutations may occur in plants that cause a change in flower color, size or other plant characteristics. And when two varieties cross-pollinate, their offspring may look like one or the other parent or a combination of the two. If the flowers appear on separate plants, this is most likely the answer.

Q I bought a croton several years ago because I liked the different colors in the leaves. Now my plant is doing well, but it generates big green leaves. Why aren't they as colorful?

Larry Smith
HUDSON, NEW HAMPSHIRE

Melinda: Crotons display the best leaf color when grown outdoors or in a sunny window indoors. All plants contain three pigments—chlorophyll (green), carotenoids (yellow and yellow-oranges) and anthocyanins (red and purple). The carotenoids and anthocyanins mask some or all of the green chlorophyll in plants with colorful leaves. In low light conditions the green chlorophyll pigment becomes more pronounced than the other two pigments. Move your plant to a sunnier window and you should see an improvement in the leaf color.

Iris

Q If different varieties of daylilies or irises are planted close together, will each plant continue to stay true to its original form? If not, how far apart should the plants be?

Barbara Wells MARINETTE, WISCONSIN

Melinda: The original plants will stay the same but due to cross-pollination (exchange of genetic material between two different varieties of daylily or iris), their offspring won't. You can avoid this problem by deadheading faded flowers. This prevents seeds from developing. Also remove the few, if any, unwanted seedlings that appear at the base of the plants. Don't worry about limiting growth. Both daylilies and irises increase in size as they grow larger root systems or rhizomes that produce more stems.

When growing daylilies or irises, it's possible to mix varieties, but stay with plants that are equally assertive. Otherwise, the more aggressive plant may engulf the other.

Did You Know?
Trumpet vines can offer hummingbirds up to 10 times more nectar than most other plants.

Q I transplanted a trumpet vine from a friend's yard that had lots of blooms. My vine has only had one bloom in several years. What's wrong with it?

Rose Seely SPENCER, NEW YORK

Melinda: I know it can be tough, but trumpet vines require patience. First and foremost, they need to reach maturity before they start blooming. This can take several years after planting. It's important to avoid high nitrogen fertilizers, because they promote leaf and stem growth while also preventing flowering. Trumpet vines develop an extensive root system that allows them to absorb nutrients from surrounding plant beds and nearby lawns. This means you need to be careful when fertilizing these areas. Use a low-nitrogen, slow-release fertilizer to increase your chance of having a beautiful, blooming vine.

Q These leaves have been growing in my yard for 20 years but have never bloomed. But then one summer a stalk produced these pretty spider lilies. Why?

Robin Downing
TALLAHASSEE, FLORIDA

Melinda: What a nice surprise. A change in the environment or the care given to this area of the landscape might explain the sudden blooms. Spider lilies (*Hymenocallis*) often fail to bloom when they are in too much shade, the soil is too dry or the plants have received too much or not enough fertilizer. Correcting one of these limiting factors may have produced blooms. Keep up with any changes in growing conditions so you can ensure your plant blooms again next year.

Q Is it possible to dig up a rosemary plant and overwinter it successfully? Mine usually brown up and wither away.

Kristie Day Bialobzeski BALLSTON LAKE, NEW YORK

Melinda: Rosemary is challenging to overwinter indoors. This Mediterranean herb thrives in bright light, cool temperatures and moist soil—all of which are usually lacking indoors during winter. Grow rosemary in containers next summer. This will make the transition from outdoors to indoors less stressful. You'll avoid root damage when digging up the plant and poor drainage when garden soil is moved into the pot. I've had great results overwintering my rosemary plants in a cool basement under artificial lights.

Q I love my begonias. Do you have some tips to keep them happy and beautiful through the winter?

Boni Trombetta WEST CHESTER, PENNSYLVANIA

Melinda: Keeping begonias healthy when moved indoors for winter is a challenge. The light intensity is lower and days are shorter in most parts of the country. Place the plants near a sunny window but away from cold drafts. Consider adding an artificial light to encourage healthy, more stout growth. Group plants together or place on pebbles in a saucer filled with water to increase humidity around the plants. Make sure the begonias are elevated above the water to avoid root rot. Give the plants plenty of space for the best light penetration, increased airflow and fewer disease problems.

Q Should I deadhead my coneflowers?

Mike Homan TOPEKA, KANSAS

Melinda: You'll have an impressive display of flowers whether you deadhead them or not. Removing faded flowers allows new blooms to shine and creates a tidier appearance. So it depends on how much effort you want to expend for your desired results. Stop deadheading in late summer to allow seedheads to develop. The seeds provide food for the birds and winter interest in the landscape. Just be aware that you'll have lots of seedlings sprouting from fallen seed in spring.

How to Deadhead

There are a couple of ways to remove spent blooms and encourage growth, depending on the size of the plant. If it has thin stalks, simply pinch the flowers off. For plants with sturdier stems, such as coneflowers, you'll need pruning shears.

Dahlia

Q Is September too late in the year to plant liatris corms and dahlia tuberous roots?

Barbara Giese
MANITOWOC, WISCONSIN

Melinda: It's best to plant liatris corms in spring or early summer. You could either store them for winter or try planting them this fall with other spring-flowering bulbs. If you decide to plant them in late summer, wait for the soil to cool so the corms do not sprout this year. Your dahlias have to wait—September is too late to plant them outside. The plants won't have time to sprout, grow and replenish energy before the first frost in your area. You could try growing the dahlias inside but most homes do not have sufficient light. I suggest storing the dahlia tuberous roots and liatris corms in a cool, dark location for winter. Pack them in peat moss to prevent the bulbs from drying out. If they're still firm and plump after the cold season has passed, plant them in spring.

LEFT TO RIGHT: THE GOATMAN/SHUTTERSTOCK; CLARA/SHUTTERSTOCK; A. ASTES/ALAMY STOCK PHOTO

Q When I started plants from seed, there were what looked like little eggs on my cleome leaves. The rest of my plants were fine. What happened to those particular cleomes?

Jen St. Louis ELMIRA, ONTARIO

Melinda: It is not a disease or insect problem but rather a physiological disorder. Basically, the plant forms these growths in response to its environment. In some cases, the plant absorbs moisture faster than it loses it, causing bumps to develop on the leaves. You often see this disorder on ivy geraniums, sweet potato vines, tomatoes and other plants. Fortunately, the problem usually corrects itself once the plants move into the garden and receive the preferred growing conditions. Until it is transplant time, continue to water and fertilize as needed. If you're using artificial lights, keep them 4 to 6 inches above the top of the plant.

Q. I planted a wisteria vine several years ago. Every year, foliage appears, but the plant doesn't produce any flowers. Why?

Barbara Mall
DINGMANS FERRY, PENNSYLVANIA

Melinda: Poor flowering is a common lament of gardeners growing wisteria. Patience is the answer—it takes up to seven years for the plant to mature and bloom.

Too much nitrogen can impede flowering and encourage rampant vine growth, so cut back on fertilizing and consider a low-nitrogen, slow-release fertilizer if you feel wisteria needs a nutrient boost.

For northern gardeners, the weather poses another additional challenge—though Chinese and Japanese wisterias are stem-hardy, cold winters may kill the flower buds. Since you can't control the weather, you'll have to have to settle for beautiful foliage most seasons.

Or try Kentucky wisteria (*Wisteria macrostachya*, below), which I've seen flowering in Zone 4; its flowers are smaller and appear on new growth. Though less showy, it may be a more reliable option.

Q. I love peonies and have bought several types in the past years, but they have no smell. The best part of peonies is their fragrance. How can I get them to smell as good as they're supposed to?

Linda Caldwell NEWPORT, VIRGINIA

Melinda: Fragrance varies from one variety of peony to the next. When selecting peonies, look for varieties that are advertised as fragrant. The red-flecked white flowers of the Festiva Maxima are considered one of the most aromatic. Flying Swallow in a Red Dress (an early bloomer) and Red Magic both have spicy fragrances. Snow Lotus' single flowers and the double-pink blossoms of Eden's Perfume also have an intense scent.

Q In early summer, small, round berries appear on my wisteria, and it has full foliage, but no blooms. What is wrong?

Bev Lutkenhaus CALMAR, IOWA

Melinda: Those little berries are likely flower buds. Late spring frosts, fluctuating temperatures and overly dry soil can prevent buds from opening or cause them to drop off the plant completely. Chances are you're growing a type of Asian wisteria—Chinese or Japanese. Some of these varieties can take more than 15 years before they bloom. Midwest gardeners usually have better success growing American wisteria (*Wisteria frutescens*). It may be a bit less spectacular than the Asian wisterias because the flowers appear with the leaves, but it is a more reliable bloomer.

Q Can I use the ashes from our winter firewood to improve my veggie garden?

Mike Murnock
McKEAN, PENNSYLVANIA

Melinda: Ash does not improve drainage in garden soil. It has a high pH so it should not be added to alkaline soils or worked in around plants like blueberries, red maples, rhododendrons and others that require acidic (low pH) soils. Have your soil tested before adding it to your garden. If the ash is from untreated wood, you can add it to the compost pile. Sprinkle some on each layer as you build your pile. The wood ash helps neutralize the acidic nature of compost. Do not use ashes from charcoal briquettes or treated wood.

Q Is there anything I can do in winter to improve my raised vegetable beds?

MaryAnne Katz PORTLAND, OREGON

Melinda: Incorporating compost into the soil adds important nutrients and organic matter that increase its water-holding ability and improve drainage. Compost also helps the health and vigor of plants, making them less vulnerable to insects and disease. Growing a green manure crop on raised beds is another way to improve the soil. To create green manure, just sow buckwheat, clover, peas or winter wheat in autumn and work the plants back into the soil next spring. It's a great way to add organic matter while crowding out unwanted cold-weather weeds. For information on green manure, research online or call your local extension office.

Backyard Tip

For best results, grow mums in a spot that gets at least 6 hours of sun per day with well-drained soil.

Q Every time I buy mums in the fall, I ask if they are winter hardy. I plant them and in the spring they never come up. What could I be doing wrong?

Linda Barnes NEW LONDON, OHIO

Melinda: You are definitely not alone in your struggle. The mums and asters we purchase in fall are in full bloom, so the plant diverts much of its energy into flowering instead of developing roots to help the plants survive the winter. Try planting mums in spring so they have time to become established before the flowering and winter season. More and more garden centers are selling mums in spring for exactly this reason.

Did You Know?
This charming purple plant is also known as purpletop vervain or tall verbena.

Q Do you have any tips for starting *Verbena bonariensis* from seed? My attempts to grow it from purchased seeds and from seed heads have failed.

Jane Fiore
COLORADO SPRINGS, COLORADO

Melinda: You are not alone in your struggle to grow this beauty from seed. Give the seeds a cold treatment in the refrigerator for two weeks prior to sprouting. Place the seeds in moistened compost in a plastic bag or just plant the seeds and place the whole container in the refrigerator. Then move to a 65-degree location for germination. Be patient, though; it can take 28 days or more for seeds to germinate. Grow seedlings in a bright location or under artificial lights with good air circulation.

Q This is the first year I'm able to harvest asparagus. Should I leave a couple of spears on each plant to grow and feed the roots for any future harvests?

Douglas Cestone
GLEN ROCK, NEW JERSEY

Melinda: Harvest all asparagus spears when they are 7 to 9 inches in size throughout the harvest period. Once the harvest period is complete, allow the shoots to form the ferny growth. Leave this intact throughout the season so it can produce energy and return it to the roots. Recent research has found that making several harvests over a few weeks the first year after planting does not harm the plants and actually encourages more budding. The second year, you can harvest for 4 to 6 weeks and the third and subsequent years harvest for about 6 to 8 weeks. By then the outdoor temperatures are usually rising, the shoots are a bit tougher and the plants form the ferny growth even faster.

Q When the pods of my amaryllis broke open, I collected the seeds. What should I do with them and how do I plant them?

Gerald Stevens PARKERSBURG, ILLINOIS

Melinda: Allow freshly collected seeds to dry for several days before planting or store the dried seeds in the refrigerator until you're ready to plant. Start with clean containers with drainage holes, filled with a sterile potting or seed starting mix. Leave the papery covering on the seeds intact and lay them on the potting mix. Cover lightly, about ⅛ of an inch, with potting mix. Keep the soil warm (about 70 to 75 degrees) and moist. Seeds should germinate within 4 to 6 weeks. The seedlings will look like a young chive plant. Move them to a sunny location or under artificial lights as soon as they appear. Keep in mind it will take several years for the plants to reach maturity and start producing flowers.

Backyard Tip
If you live in Zones 8 to 10, you can grow amaryllis bulbs directly in the ground in full sun.

Q How do I transplant vining passionflower?

Sally Brooks LAVERNIA, TEXAS

Melinda: You can dig and transplant your passionflower in fall after it has gone dormant, or in early spring before growth begins. Dig a trench around the plant larger than the desired root ball.

Then use a sharp shovel or loppers to cut any large roots. Slide a piece of burlap under the root ball to transport and contain the roots. Lift and move your passionflower to its new location. Set the plant in the pre-dug hole, remove or cut back the burlap and plant at the same level where it was growing before.

Another option is to dig and transplant runners. Use a sharp spade to cut through the underground root-like rhizome. Lift and replant in a container or the desired location. Cuttings and layering are also effective ways to start new plants.

Q Why do the pods on my wisteria burst open? It's the strangest sound!

Barbara Archibald
PAOLI, PENNSYLVANIA

Melinda: This is completely normal for wisteria. When the seeds are ripe, the pods explode, dispersing the seeds far from the parent plant. Jewelweed and witch hazel also disperse their seeds this way. Other plants use different methods to disperse seeds. Some have fluffy seeds that are carried by wind, others drop their seeds in water. Those like burdock have prickly seeds that stick to animal fur or our clothing to be spread beyond their current location.

Q. My mother used to successfully grow rose cuttings under a jar. However, I have not had any luck. How can I grow a rose this way?

Dick Milosovic MACEDONIA, OHIO

Melinda: Parents and grandparents often have that magical ability to make anything root and grow, don't they? You can start by taking a 4- to 6-inch cutting from roses that are about to bloom or have just bloomed. Remove any flowers and buds. Dip the cut end in a rooting hormone to encourage rooting and discourage disease. Stick the rose cutting in a container filled with a well-drained potting mix. Keep the soil moist and the container out of direct sunlight. Loosely cover with plastic to increase the humidity as the cutting develops roots. In 4 to 8 weeks the cutting should be rooted and ready to move into the garden or a new container.

Monarch on a
purple coneflower

Q. I've been having difficulty growing coneflowers and zinnias. Any advice you can give me on how to make them thrive in my garden?

Sierra Conine EL DORADO, KANSAS

Melinda: Start by reviewing your growing conditions. Both of these plants prefer full sun and will tolerate dry soils once established. If you find that your conditions are appropriate, the problem could be disease. Both these plants are susceptible to a disease called aster yellows, which is transferred from infected plants to healthy ones by the aster yellow leafhopper. The disease can stunt the plants and distort and discolor the flowers. Remove infected plants as soon as you see them to prevent the disease from spreading to healthy plants. Sanitation is the only control option. Controlling the leafhopper with an insecticide labeled for use on these plants may help to reduce the leafhopper population and ultimately slow the spread of the disease.

Q Every spring when the iris (*Iris pseudacorus*) in my fish pool blooms, the flowers stay wedged in the base of the leaves instead of coming up on stems. What causes this?

Irene Holzman PENSACOLA, FLORIDA

Melinda: Environmental stress can cause the stunting of flower stalks. Make sure the rhizomes have plenty of room to grow. Excessive heat and sun in hot climates like yours can also stress these plants. Be sure to remove seedpods as they start to develop. Doing so helps reduce the energy spent on forming seeds, but more importantly, it helps to prevent the spread of this invasive plant into natural waterways.

Q I can't seem to get hens-and-chicks to grow. I have tried for several years and still fail. What can I do to keep them alive?

Bonnie Partridge OLIVET, MICHIGAN

Melinda: Hens-and-chicks grow best in full sun and well-drained soils. Gardeners who have heavy clay and poorly drained soils struggle to keep these and other succulents alive. Try growing them in a container filled with a well-drained potting mix. When cold weather hits, move potted hens-and-chicks into an unheated garage or bury the pot in the ground for winter to insulate the roots against your cold temperatures.

Backyard Tip
Have a little fun growing hens-and-chicks in containers. We often see readers planting them in old shoes or purses!

9 Steps to Growing a Greener Backyard

Adopt earth-friendly habits and your yard (and wallet) will thank you.

By Rachael Liska

Plant perennial wildflowers instead of a typical lawn for a healthy green space.

Build time into your morning routine for watering plants.

T PAYS TO BE GREEN, whether it's because you want to live an environmentally conscious lifestyle or you simply want to save time and money. No matter your motives, your backyard will be better for it. Here are a few tips for transforming your space from good to great.

1. Don't mow as deep

Try letting your lawn grow a few inches to help it better tolerate drought conditions in warmer months. (Cool-season grasses can grow up to 3½ to 4 inches, while most warm-season grasses are shorter.) Roots grow deeper and lawns thicker, which means fewer pests, less disease and a decreased need for chemical intervention.

2. Grow local

Native plants are accustomed to their area's growing conditions, so they're a smart low-maintenance option. Once established, they generally require less water and have fewer pest and disease problems. Native wildlife love them, too, as they're a fantastic source for food and shelter. Check with your local nursery or extension service to see which species are appropriate for the growing conditions in your neck of the woods.

3. Water the right way

Water between 6 and 10 a.m., when the air is cool and not as much moisture will be lost to evaporation. Watering in late afternoon is the next best option. Be sure that foliage has time to dry before damp nighttime temperatures (and fungal diseases) set in. Water near the base of plants rather than overhead—soaker hoses are ideal, as they save water by slowly delivering the good stuff right to the roots. For lawns, water long and deep (an inch should do) once a week.

4. Get keen on composting

It's not called "gardener's gold" for nothing. Compost keeps kitchen leftovers out of landfills and enriches soil with much-needed nutrients. Not only does it reduce dependency on chemical fertilizers, but compost also improves drainage, water retention and soil texture. Veggie and fruit scraps, tea bags, coffee grounds, eggshells, shredded newspaper, dry leaves and untreated grass clippings are all fair game. To get started, check out *birdsandblooms.com/composting*.

5. Opt for outdoor furniture that's earth-friendly

When shopping for wood benches or tables, check to make sure they are certified as sustainable.

Bee balm is a pollinator magnet for attracting bees, butterflies and more.

A hardwood like acacia, which grows in abundance and is considered invasive in many regions, and wood such as teak, from plantations managed for long-term preservation, are good choices. The same goes for patio sets made from recycled aluminum or plastic.

6. Save with solar lighting

Make the backyard as beautiful in the dark as it is in the daytime with night-lights. With earth-friendly solar-powered spotlights, deck lights and path lights available in various sizes, it's easy to find a style that suits your landscape. They don't need wires or extension cords, so you can put them in any sunny spot.

7. Grow to be wild

Trade in the mower for some mulch. Take a corner of your lawn and replace it with a bed of pretty native plants or mulch that can be used to anchor a kids play set. Plant a fairy garden full of frilly ferns in an area that receives a lot of shade, or try a rain garden in a low-lying spot of waterlogged lawn. Living in the desert? Use cactus and stone to build a beautiful yet rugged water-efficient xeriscape.

8. Mulch fall leaves with your lawn mower

Forget all that raking, blowing and bagging. Let fall leaves lie, and cut them into tiny bits with a mulching lawn mower instead. Not only does this save your back, but also the shredded leaves add nutrients to the soil as they decompose. Shred leaves when grass is poking through them (don't let the leaves completely bury the grass, though). If you don't have a mulching mower, look into a leaf vacuum with mulching capabilities.

9. Welcome pollinators

According to the U.S. Fish & Wildlife Service, pollinators such as honeybees, butterflies and hummingbirds help pollinate 75% of our flowering plants and nearly 75% of our crops. There is increasing evidence that many of these vital pollinators are in decline. Planting a garden that includes plants that flower at different times of the year will provide nectar and pollen sources for pollinators throughout the growing season. Whenever possible, choose native plants in a variety of flower colors and shapes. See *fws.gov/pollinators* for more important information.

Layering for Success
Lettuce and cabbage thrive when planted using the lasagna gardening method.

Quick Fixes for Poor Soil

Layer your way to a more productive garden in just one season.

By Melinda Myers

WHETHER YOU'RE converting grass to a garden or creating a brand-new planting area as a result of recent construction, the soil probably needs a little elbow grease and TLC.

Incorporating compost or other organic matter into the top foot of your soil improves drainage in yards with heavy clay deposits and helps sandy or rocky plots hold water better. While this process yields healthy plants, it takes decades of yearly maintenance to make a difference. Luckily, a few remedies start to work almost immediately.

Purchasing topsoil and creating new beds on top of your current soil is a less time-consuming alternative. Despite this quick fix, many gardeners end up with weed-filled, poor-draining topsoil that's worse than what they started with. Always consult friends or family who have found a reliable source before purchasing any topsoil.

Boosting poor soil with recycled materials from your own yard may be a more cost-effective and productive solution.

One way to get richer soil is lasagna gardening. As the name suggests, you build new garden beds with lasagna-like layers of plant-based materials, alternating brown ones (rich in carbon) and green ones (rich in nitrogen) with tiers of compost.

To start construction, mark the outline of the garden. Then lay down a layer of newspaper or cardboard to suppress any weeds and existing grass. Wet the newspaper to keep it on the grass as you build the garden, especially on windy days. Next, add 2 to 3 inches of compost or peat moss and then cover with 4 to 8 inches of compostable materials, such as fall leaves, vegetable kitchen scraps, herbicide-free grass clippings and other organic matter. Top it off with an inch of compost and then sprinkle on a low-nitrogen fertilizer that releases slowly. Keep layering until the bed is $1\frac{1}{2}$ to 2 feet high. Plant a garden now or build a bed in fall and plant the following spring.

Hugelkultur is another excellent soil-building option. In this method the first layer consists of logs and branches. The wood will absorb moisture and slowly release nutrients over the years, supporting the garden just as fallen branches do in the forest. Avoid cedar and black locust, which are slow to break down, and black walnut, which is toxic to other plants.

After you put down the logs and branches, build additional layers with carbon-rich materials like leaves and straw. Then top it off with a nitrogen-rich layer and several inches of a compost-enhanced topsoil. As with the lasagna method, plant immediately or wait until the following season.

Investing a little time and energy in your plot can result in a bountiful harvest and beautiful garden from the start. Both methods provide years of benefits—and in the case of *hugelkultur*, even decades.

Gather the Good Stuff
Use a combination of green and brown material to boost soil.

Green (nitrogen): Plant-based kitchen scraps, herbicide-free grass clippings, worm castings, manure, vegetable clippings, seaweed and kelp.

Brown (carbon): Cornstalks and cobs, evergreen needles, paper, branches and twigs, fall leaves, straw and hay.

CHAPTER 5

Trees & Shrubs

The workhorses of the landscape, shrubs and trees promise years of beauty as long as you properly care for them. Discover growing advice, pruning tips, plant suggestions and more!

Q After winter, only one of my snowball plants has leaves on it and just a few shoots are coming up from the roots of the plant. Do I have to take it up?

Barbara Narducci SOMERDALE, NEW JERSEY

Melinda: Several plants go by the common name of snowball. Whichever plant you have, it sounds as if the top growth was killed by winter weather. Fluctuating and extremely cold temperatures can cause dieback on plants. Prune any brittle (dead) stems back to a healthy bud or shoot, or to ground level. Allow the living stems to grow and wait to see if they thrive. If they do, you can eventually shape the new growth into an attractive plant. If not, you may want to replace it with something new. Always avoid late-season pruning and fertilization, which might stimulate late growth that will be vulnerable in winter.

Q Last winter, after severe weather left about 15 inches of snow on the ground, I checked on my plants and found a new blossom on my scraggly old honeysuckle bush. How did that happen?

Lowell Lehman
SPOKANE, WASHINGTON

Melinda: Plants are truly amazing. Bad weather followed by a natural winter thaw or by artificial heat from a dryer vent, reflected heat from light-colored siding or radiant heat from your house's south-side foundation might have caused buds to break and grow. Fortunate situations such as this are always photoworthy and provide a welcome pop of color in an otherwise drab winter backyard.

Backyard Tip
Applying too much nitrogen fertilizer to fruit trees can prevent flowering and fruiting.

Q. Twelve years ago, I bought two different types of apple trees because they needed pollination. I have never gotten so much as a blossom, let alone an apple. What is wrong?
Roger Boomsma
HUDSONVILLE, MICHIGAN

Melinda: Overfertilization and improper pruning can prevent flowering and fruiting. Apple and other fruit trees should be properly pruned to develop a strong open framework that allows air and light to penetrate the canopy. Light is essential for flowering and fruit development. Consult your local extension service website for guidelines on pruning apple trees. You might also consider a soil test, which your extension service can help with as well. A soil test will tell you if any fertilizer is needed, how much and what type.

Q My lilac starts off green and healthy, but then turns brown and it looks as if it's dying. A couple of weeks later, it looks healthy again. The process repeats three or four times throughout the summer. What's going on?

Robert Snyder COLUMBUS, OHIO

Melinda: Those symptoms could be a response to periods of drought. Closely examine the leaves throughout the season, monitor rainfall and irrigation practices, and see if you notice a correlation between the two.

A nutrient deficiency also causes leaf discoloration. It usually expresses itself in a certain pattern or portion of the plant. If this sounds like a possibility, have your soil tested to help you determine which, if any, fertilizer is needed. Nutrient deficiencies also occur when the soil is too wet or too dry. In these cases the plants are unable to absorb nutrients from the soil. Proper watering helps if this is the cause.

Q I have six David Austin English roses in my yard. A couple of them have blooms that droop over and hang almost upside-down. What causes this?

Gayle Romines
GREENBACKVILLE, VIRGINIA

Melinda: Large rose blossoms, common on many David Austin roses, often nod or droop. This does vary with varieties. As the plant matures and stems become thicker, the plant provides better support for the blossoms and the drooping is less noticeable. Prune the plants by no more than half in the winter, and fertilize twice a year with a low-nitrogen, organically based fertilizer. These important steps will promote sturdy growth without interfering with flowering.

Q Should I remove the snow from drooping evergreen branches?

Juli Seyfried CINCINNATI, OHIO

Melinda: You can gently brush snow off branches after each snowfall, just avoid shaking snow off the branches. This can do more damage than the wet, heavy snow. Leave the snow in place if it's frozen to the branches. Next year, do a bit of prevention to minimize weather damage to your evergreens. Wrap multistemmed arborvitaes and junipers with bird netting or strips of cotton cloth. These hold the stems together so snow rolls off the plant instead of bending the stems.

Q My lilac bushes have never bloomed. They get some direct sun, but some shade. The soil is acidic because of pine and oak trees. Is this the problem?

Joanne Eastman LOVELL, MAINE

Melinda: Evergreen needles and oak leaves have little to no impact on soil acidity. Plus, acidic soil would cause leaf discoloration and stunted growth, not merely a lack of flowers. The shade from these trees may be the culprit. Lilacs flower best with at least six hours of direct sunlight. Too much high-nitrogen fertilizer and improper pruning can also result in a lack of flowers. Go easy on the fertilizing, and prune only if needed right after the lilacs should have bloomed. These plants develop their flower buds in the summer, and the buds then open into showy blooms the following spring.

Q Which shrubs should I cover for winter?

Robin Evans EXPORT, PENNSYLVANIA

Melinda: Broadleaf evergreens are the most susceptible to winter damage in colder regions such as yours. Hemlocks, less hardy and newly planted needled evergreens, and shrubs exposed to drying winds and winter sun also benefit from protection. Create a wind break and a bit of shade with burlap or landscape fabric. Mount the fabric on stakes or posts placed on the windy and sunny side of the plants. Other options include decorative fencing, a plant protector or shrub jacket!

Further reduce winter damage to shrubs by keeping them healthy throughout the growing season. And lastly, water your shrubs thoroughly before the ground freezes.

Q I cut down most of the black walnut trees near my garden, added topsoil and rototilled, but my plants still wilt. What should I do next?

Sarah Tims
SPRINGFIELD CENTER, NEW YORK

Melinda: It takes at least five years for the roots, leaf litter and nut husks of black walnut trees to decompose fully and no longer pose a threat to susceptible plants. The roots of the remaining black walnuts can spread several hundred feet away from the trunk of the tree. As your new plantings mature and their roots grow, they may come in contact with remaining tree remnants or the roots of existing trees. Time will take care of the debris from removed trees!

For now, consider growing resistant plants. You can find plenty of examples on arboreta websites.

Black
Chokeberry

Q What bushes offer good fall color and also attract birds?

Jennifer Broadstreet Hess
MARION, KANSAS

Melinda: Shrubs provide a great opportunity to end the season in a blaze of color, and many also provide food and shelter for birds. Chokeberry has beautiful red fall color and features red or black berries that persist into winter or until the birds gobble them up. Smaller serviceberries can be treated as shrubs. They produce fruit in June and have stunning color in the fall. Many viburnums, including our native American arrowhead and blackhaw viburnums, produce food and have attractive autumn color. And don't forget about roses. Some fade to a pretty yellow color that contrasts with the tasty rose hips.

Did You Know?
You can get blue hydrangeas by using acidic soil.

Q. My hydrangeas are about 15 years old and have bloomed only once. I feed them and mulch them with pine needles and leaves in the winter. What am I doing wrong?

Loretta McClincy
BELLEFONTE, PENNSYLVANIA

Melinda: Sounds as if you have a bigleaf (*Hydrangea macrophylla*), also known as mophead hydrangea, which flowers pink in alkaline soil and blue in acidic soil. These plants bloom on the previous season's growth. So if they die back to the ground or are pruned to the ground in late winter, they will not flower.

Consider putting evergreen boughs or weed-free straw over the plants after the ground freezes. These mulches provide better insulation than leaves. In spring, remove the mulch and wait to see if there's any growth on the stems. This is the growth that will flower. You should prune off only the dead portions of the stems. If you're growing one of the repeat-blooming bigleaf hydrangeas, make sure the soil is moist, and fertilize with a low-nitrogen organic fertilizer once in spring. These varieties are supposed to flower on old and new growth with proper care.

Q My Alfredo viburnum faces southwest and looks healthy, but it does not produce any flowers, fruit or purple foliage yet. Why?

Maureen Berry LINN CREEK, MISSOURI

Melinda: Flowering shrubs such as Alfredo viburnum often direct energy to producing roots instead of flowers and fruit for the first few years. Once established, they flower and fruit more reliably. Alfredo is known for its outstanding fall color and aphid resistance. Some gardeners say it produces wonderful flowers and fruit, while other experts say they tend to be more sparse.

Overfertilization and shade also interfere with flowering and fruit, as well as fall color. If this is happening to your plant, stop fertilizing unless a soil test or the plant's growth indicates that a nutrient boost is necessary. Also take note of the shrub's location in your yard. Make sure the plant gets at least partial sun to encourage flowers, fruit and the best fall color.

Q I bought a New Dawn rose. How should I overwinter it? Do I need to wrap it in burlap?

Rebecca Williamson BUSHNELL, ILLINOIS

Melinda: This hardy climbing rose has survived the rigors of Midwest winters without any special protection. The most important thing is to keep the plant healthy throughout the growing season, water as needed until the ground freezes and stop harvesting flowers in late summer so the plant begins hardening off for the winter season. If you do that, you shouldn't have any problems!

Q Last spring, only the bottom of my 15-year-old birch tree had leaves. The upper branches were green and flexible, so I don't think they were dead. There was also dark sap running down the trunk. What happened to my tree?

Cindy Ortmann BISMARCK, NORTH DAKOTA

Melinda: Bronze birch borer is the most common pest of paper bark birches. The wormlike borer feeds under the tree bark, and the feeding eventually blocks the flow of water and nutrients to the tree's leaves and branches. This results in stunted growth, defoliation and dieback, starting at the top. To confirm borer presence, look for D-shaped exit holes and raised areas on the branches and trunk. The oozing red sap is another indication of an infestation.

Severely infested trees with more than one-third dieback may be difficult to save. A mild infestation is treatable with a systemic insecticide labeled for bronze birch borer. Consider hiring a certified arborist (*treesaregood.com* is a reliable resource) who has access to effective chemicals and equipment, and the experience to treat for this pest.

Q I have two large maple trees. I want to plant flowers because grass doesn't grow well under the trees. Can I?

Roberta Roselli
JAMESTOWN, NEW YORK

Melinda: A lack of sunlight and water prevents plants from growing under trees with dense canopies, but drought- and shade-tolerant ground covers can provide some color in this situation. Do not add topsoil under the canopy of your trees. Even just an inch of additional soil can weaken and kill the trees over time. Instead, plant perennial ground covers in the existing soil and mulch with shredded bark or wood chips. Water often to keep the roots moist for the first few years. Once established, these ground covers are usually more drought-tolerant.

You can also set pots of annual flowers on the soil surface in the ground cover or a mulched bed for added seasonal color. Or, sink a few old nursery pots in the ground. Plant your annuals in a slightly smaller container and set it inside the buried pot to make it look as though the annuals are growing in the ground.

Q My forsythia bloomed in fall. Will it bloom again in spring?

Debbie Sharkey JUNEAU, WISCONSIN

Melinda: I often see forsythia, lilac and other spring-blooming trees produce flowers in the fall. Extreme temperature fluctuations, drought or other stressful growing conditions can trick the plants into thinking they went through the dormant period, causing them to bloom. Buds that flower this late in the year, unfortunately, won't bloom next spring.

Backyard Tip
Before planting this butterfly magnet, make sure it's not invasive in your area.

Q How can I keep butterfly bushes alive through winter in Zone 6a? I have sadly lost one plant per year for the past four years.
Connie Mason Etter
MARTINSVILLE, INDIANA

Melinda: Keep trying! I am a Zone 5a gardener and have had success with butterfly bushes, both in a small city lot and now in a more brutal open, rural location. Grow these plants in a sunny, well-draining spot. Avoid late-season fertilization, because it promotes growth that is likely to be killed by winter weather. Leave the plants standing to increase hardiness and provide winter interest. Cut them back to 4 to 6 inches above the ground in late winter or early spring, before growth begins. Then be patient. Mine have sprouted as late as mid-July after an extremely cold winter and cool spring. The bushes quickly reached full size and were covered with blooms and butterflies by early August. Well worth the wait!

Keep It Tidy
All climbing roses, including this Bathsheba English rose, need to be groomed often. Remove damaged or dead leaves from bushes and the surrounding ground to keep plants disease-free.

Q. Should I cut back my climbing roses in spring, in fall or not at all?

Nancy Griepentrog
WATERLOO, WISCONSIN

Melinda: If your roses bloom only once a year, wait to prune until right after they flower. Prune reblooming climbers in early spring before growth begins. Remove any dead, diseased or very old canes back to ground level for both types of plants. Cut side branches back 3 to 6 inches, leaving at least three or four buds to encourage more flowering. Train these shoots to grow horizontally for even more blossoms the following year.

Q I have a cherry tree that produces leaves in the spring but starts dropping them in July. In October, blooms and foliage appear until frost. Is it common for a cherry tree to bloom but have no fruit?

Dorina DeVaughn
LENOIR CITY, TENNESSEE

Melinda: Stressful weather, leaf spot diseases and insect infestations cause trees to drop their leaves prematurely. Often the plant is tricked into a false dormancy, blooming off-season as it recovers from the stress. A lack of a compatible pollinator, poor bee activity or frost can prevent the pollination a fruit tree needs for fruit to form. Take a look at the fallen leaves for clues to the cause. Consult your local extension office for solutions.

Q Should I remove the burlap wrap before I plant a new tree?

MaryAnne Katz PORTLAND, OREGON

Melinda: There's a great deal of debate among arborists as to whether you should keep or remove the burlap. Some nurseries void their guarantee if you remove the burlap at planting. Always remove treated burlap that does not decay in the soil. I prefer to cut away the burlap wrap and wire cages once the tree is settled in the planting hole. This minimizes disturbances of the rootball. Minimally, you should remove the twine and peel back the burlap so it is not exposed to the air. Burlap acts as a wick, moving moisture from the soil surrounding the tree roots to the surface, where it evaporates into the air.

Q Which trees and shrubs should I prune or cut back in early winter? Which should be left alone until late winter or early spring?

Jen St. Louis ELMIRA, ONTARIO

Melinda: Always prune with a purpose, whether it's to establish a strong framework, remove damaged and hazardous branches, encourage flowering and fruiting, or manage growth. Timing depends on the type of plant.

- **Spring-blooming shrubs**: Prune right after flowering to maintain early flowers while controlling growth.
- **Summer-blooming shrubs:** Prune any time during the dormant season—I prefer late winter or early spring before growth begins. Correct winter damage then, too. Pruning wounds close quickly as new growth begins in spring.
- **Evergreen shrubs:** Prune in later winter. They suffer less damage if the tender inner growth is not exposed until the worst of winter weather has passed.
- **Pine trees:** Prune in spring as the buds elongate into what we call candles. These are cut to limit new growth.
- **Spruce trees:** Prune above healthy buds or adjoining branches in spring before growth begins.

Wiegela (pink) and Ninebark (white)

Q I planted three perennial hibiscus shrubs, and I've read conflicting stories about pruning and winterizing. What is the right way to care for them?

Kathryn Small SIMPSONVILLE, KENTUCKY

Melinda: I assume you are speaking of *Hibiscus syriacus*, commonly called rose of Sharon or shrub Althea. It is hardy in Zones 5 to 8 or 9, although it may suffer severe injury or death when temperatures dip to 20 degrees below zero. Proper siting and care should be sufficient to prepare these plants for your winter. Prune young plants to encourage balanced growth and branching if needed. Once established, these plants need minimal pruning. Just remove any winter dieback. Because this plant blooms on new growth, it can be pruned any time during the dormant season. I prefer late winter or early spring before growth begins. That way you can remove any winter injury while managing the size and shape of the plant.

Small-Space Favorites

A typical rose of Sharon shrub reaches about 12 feet high and 10 feet wide, but dwarf options offer a more petite habit. Try Lil' Kim, which has white flowers with a red center, or Pollypetite (pictured above)—both reach 4 feet tall.

Q Lately I've noticed dead limbs and almost no fruit on my 10-year-old loquat tree. There is a large live oak nearby. Is there any hope at all for the tree?

Richard Merriam TAMPA, FLORIDA

Melinda: Lack of light and competition for water from the live oak may be the problem. Water the tree thoroughly whenever the top few inches of soil start to dry. Be vigilant about watering, especially during fruit development and extended dry periods. Use shredded leaves from the oak as a soil mulch to conserve moisture, suppress weeds and improve the soil as the leaves decompose. The leaves are not toxic to other plants. You can also try surrounding the loquat tree with a 3-inch layer of wood chip or bark mulch. Pull the mulch away from the trunk to avoid problems. If this doesn't do the trick, it may be time to move the tree or plant a new one in a sunnier location.

Q I want to plant pecan and peach trees. Is fall a good time to plant?

Roylan Neill Sullivan OZONA, TEXAS

Melinda: In Texas, people typically plant fruit and nut trees during the dormant season because the soil is warm and the air is cool. This gives plants time to get established in the ground before hot weather moves in. Plant fruit and nut trees that were grown in containers whenever they are available; you will just need to be more vigilant when planting during the warmer months. Be sure to mulch the soil around the trees and to water thoroughly when the top few inches are crumbly and moist.

Invincibelle Spirit
hydrangea

Backyard Tip
For more hydrangea options, try growing Annabelle cultivars, such as Invincibelle Spirit or Bella Anna, which produce showy pink blooms on new growth.

Q How can I get my hydrangeas to bloom each year? And how can I protect them in winter as they get bigger?

Phyllis Foster FREDERICKTOWN, OHIO

Melinda: Most bigleaf hydrangeas, those with pink or blue flowers, produce blooms only on the previous season's growth. In your climate, you need to protect the future flowering stems from the cold. Try encircling the plant with 4-foot-tall hardware cloth. Sink it several inches into the ground to keep out rabbits and voles, then fill with weed-free straw or evergreen boughs to insulate the plant. Wrapping the fencing with burlap or weed barrier will add another layer of insulation.

Many northern gardeners have given up on these plants and switched to the hardier panicle hydrangeas, whose flowers start out white and fade to pink before turning brown. The Endless Summer hydrangea collection is supposed to bloom on new and old growth. Moisture and proper fertilization are the keys to success with these.

LEFT: BLICKWINKEL/ALAMY STOCK PHOTO; FAR RIGHT: PETER RIDWELL

Q My Rustica Rubra Saucer magnolia bloomed twice within a year and then produced seedpods for the first time. Is this unusual?

Jim Flindall ST. CATHARINES, ONTARIO

Melinda: Plants often bloom out of their normal cycle when they experience unusual weather. Drought or temperatures that are cooler than normal can trigger some spring-flowering plants to bloom again in summer or fall. Saucer magnolias rarely form seedpods. Stressful weather conditions can stimulate seed formation. Continue providing proper care and your tree will be fine, although it may have fewer flowers next spring.

Q Will this Alberta spruce survive?

Janice Smalley
WISCONSIN DELLS, WISCONSIN

Melinda: Yes, the plant will survive, but it may take years to regain its former beauty, if it ever does. The winter winds that typically blow in from the northwest and winter sun from the south cause the needles of this and many evergreens to brown. The needles continue to lose moisture throughout the winter, while the frozen soil prevents the roots from absorbing water. The best thing you can do for your evergreens is water all new and existing plantings thoroughly before the ground freezes.

Q Our rose of Sharon tree drops its seeds, and now our lawn is full of tiny trees. I am constantly picking them out and weed killer didn't work! How can we get rid of these pests, short of cutting the tree down?

PATRICIA MORABITO NORTHLAKE, ILLINOIS

Melinda: If it's any consolation, many gardeners suffer the same plight. Older rose of Sharon varieties lost favor because of these nuisance seedlings. Newer ones such as Helene are sterile, eliminating this pesky problem.

With your current tree, prevent these nuisance seedlings with a bit of deadheading. Remove the faded flowers and the developing seedpod at the base before they have a chance to form seeds. It takes some time, but it's less tedious than digging hundreds of seedlings out of the lawn. If you choose to use a chemical, look for one of the woody plant weed killers labeled for this purpose. Consider spot-treating or painting the chemical on the unwanted seedlings to minimize the impact on the environment. As always, read and follow label directions carefully.

Q. I have tried many times to grow avocado trees from pits. Although the pits sprout in water, not one of the plants has survived longer than six months after I transplant them into soil. What am I doing wrong?

Christa Pederson DULUTH, MINNESOTA

Melinda: Try these techniques to increase success when growing any young plant indoors. Always use a container with drainage holes. Use a quality potting mix; soil from the garden does not drain well when placed in a container, and it may contain insects and disease organisms detrimental to your plant's health. Move rooted cuttings and sprouted seeds into a container slightly larger than the root system, as placing small plants in a much larger pot can lead to root rot.

Wash an Avocado Seed

Then use three toothpicks to suspend it, broad-end down, half covered with water in a glass. See how long it takes to sprout!

LEFT: ANEST/ISTOCK; RIGHT: DOREENWYNJA.COM

Prune Like a Pro
Study the shape of the plant before making any cuts and make sure you always use clean, sharp tools. Avoid overpruning by cutting only a fourth to a third of the canopy per year.

Q I have a 7-year-old oakleaf hydrangea in a shaded location. It grows a lot of healthy foliage that I have to prune regularly, but it bloomed only once or twice. Why do you think that is?

William Stovall
CHARLESTON, SOUTH CAROLINA

Melinda: It's all about the timing when pruning this and other hydrangeas. Oakleaf hydrangeas produce flower buds the year before they bloom. Keep pruning to a minimum to maximize the floral display. Remove only the damaged and wayward branches each year as needed. This helps control the plant's size while encouraging it to bloom. Heavy pruning stimulates growth and results in a larger plant that needs additional pruning. Selective pruning leaves you with more stems with intact flower buds for a better bloom the following year.

TREES & SHRUBS **147**

Did You Know?

Spirea does not love shade. It'll tolerate some, but performs best in full sun.

Q My spirea plants are in full sun and get normal amounts of water. They appear to be turning brown and partially dying. Is water the problem?

Donald Thurlow WHITEHOUSE, TEXAS

Melinda: Too much and too little water could be causing the dieback you describe. Water thoroughly when the top few inches of soil are dry. Make sure water is draining away, not collecting around the roots of the plant. Use a pipe to remove a plug of soil or carefully dig down near the plant to check drainage. Adjust the amount of water or consider moving the plant to an area with better drainage if needed.

Q How can I get the seeds of Gabriel's trumpet to germinate? I've tried soaking, nicking and freezing them from recent to older seed harvests, to no avail.

Ted Lloyd OTTAWA, ONTARIO

Melinda: Gabriel's trumpet is one of several common names for Brugmansia. Others may know it as angel's trumpet. Most varieties are not self-fertile, meaning they need to be pollinated by another variety for seed to form. This also means their offspring will likely be different from the parent plant. Follow these steps:

1. **Collect seeds from dried pods.** The seeds inside the prickly pod have a corky covering.
2. **Soak the seeds 24 to 48 hours before planting.** Then remove the corky covering. Soaking the seeds will soften them, making the removal of the covering easier and allowing for germination.
3. **Plant the seeds a quarter inch below the soil surface in sterile, well-drained potting or seed-starting mix.** The seeds and leaves are highly toxic if ingested, so handle plants and store seeds with care. Be patient; the seeds may not sprout for several weeks to over a month.

Q I have trouble overwintering my shrubs in containers. I water them well in fall and they're sheltered. What am I doing wrong?

Monica Hildebrant CRANBROOK, BRITISH COLUMBIA

Melinda: Cold temperatures and dry soil may be the problem. Since pots contain a small volume of soil and are surrounded by the winter air, they dry out faster and the temperature is colder than it would be if the plants were in the ground. Make sure the container is weatherproof, and insulate the roots by surrounding the pots with mulch, bales of straw or bags of leaves. Also, be sure to water the plants any time the soil is thawed and dry.

Sunjoy Citrus barberry

Fragrant white
flowers cover
American plum
trees before late
summer's shiny
red fruit arrives.

Branch Out with Blooms

Perk up spring landscapes with any of these 14 native flowering trees.

By Heather Lamb

F**OR YEARS,** I worked in an office with a window overlooking woods. Each spring I'd watch as yellow daffodils emerged along the trees' edge, but for me, the new season didn't start until the lone redbud bloomed. Its rose-pink glow amid the leafless trees felt like hope after a long winter.

Flowering trees often signal the return of spring. Combine that with the trees' typically smaller stature, and they are ideal for home landscapes. This list includes 14 suggestions, all North American natives.

American plum

PRUNUS AMERICANA

This wild plum thrives across a huge swath of North America and occurs naturally in woodlands and along roadsides. In early spring its white, fragrant flowers emerge, followed by large, edible fruit. Untended, it can become a thorny thicket, but it will grow upright with care.

WHITE FLOWERS; 15 TO 25 FEET TALL; ZONES 3 TO 8

Flowering crabapple

MALUS

When I moved to Missouri, I was thrilled to discover a flowering crabapple in our new yard. The trees are abundant in northern areas, but I'd never had one of my own. Its lavish buds typically are pink when closed but open to white blooms. Once plagued by disease, crabapple's dozens of cultivars now offer disease resistance, varied flower colors (including pink) and tree sizes.

WHITE OR PINK FLOWERS; 10 TO 25 FEET TALL; ZONES 4 TO 8

Extremely popular in the North, crabapple trees provide four seasons of backyard interest.

Washington hawthorn
CRATAEGUS PHAENOPYRUM

Although often grown for its fruit, this hawthorn variety is a worthy choice for its white spring flowers as well. (But fair warning: Many find the scent unpleasant. It also has thorns!) The tree grows into a broad oval shape and withstands heat better than other hawthorns.

WHITE FLOWERS; 25 TO 30 FEET TALL; ZONES 4 TO 8

Eastern redbud
CERCIS CANADENSIS

With deep pink blooms that glaze its leafless branches in early spring, and a low, horizontal form that is downright dashing, redbuds are a popular and versatile choice in eastern gardens. A western version called Greene California redbud (*Cercis orbiculata*) is similarly attractive.

ROSE-PINK FLOWERS; 20 TO 30 FEET TALL; ZONES 4 TO 9

Flowering dogwood
CORNUS FLORIDA

If crabapple is the go-to choice for northern gardeners, flowering dogwood is similarly sentimental in the South. The dogwood's low, horizontal branches and unmistakable flowers make it a classic, though it's not as plentiful as it once was because the trees aren't long-lived and are susceptible to disease. Plant in partial shade and moist, acidic and well-drained soil to keep the trees healthy. Pacific dogwood (*Cornus nuttallii*) is the species suited to the West Coast.

WHITE FLOWERS; 20 FEET TALL; ZONES 5 TO 9
(*C. NUTTALLII*: 20 TO 30 FEET TALL; ZONES 7 TO 9)

Sweetbay magnolia
MAGNOLIA VIRGINIANA

The buds of sweetbay magnolia are less susceptible to frost because the tree blooms later

A prothonotary warbler perches in a native flowering dogwood tree.

in spring than its relatives. Once they emerge, the flowers live up to the family's reputation: They are creamy white, fragrant and large (2 to 3 inches). Native to areas prone to flooding, this magnolia often is multistemmed and remains relatively small.

WHITE FLOWERS; 10 TO 20 FEET TALL; ZONES 5 TO 9

Desert willow

CHILOPSIS LINEARIS

This native of the Southwest tolerates heat but doesn't do well in wet conditions. Despite the name, the tree isn't part of the willow family; it's kin with catalpas and trumpet vines. The tree has multiple trunks and an airy habit. Its pink or white flowers open in late spring and continue through August.

WHITE OR PINK FLOWERS; 15 TO 25 FEET TALL; ZONES 7 TO 9

Downy serviceberry

AMELANCHIER ARBOREA

Growing up, we called this tree a Juneberry, and my brother and I would join my mom in early summer to collect its fruit into old ice cream buckets. The downy is a good serviceberry selection for its ability to withstand varied soil types and conditions. The racemes of white flowers, though short-lived, are showy and appear in midspring.

WHITE FLOWERS; 15 TO 25 FEET TALL; ZONES 4 TO 9

Tulip poplar

LIRIODENDRON TULIPIFERA

Named for its tulip-shaped leaves and tuliplike flowers, everything about this tree is grand. It grows up to 90 feet tall. Its stunning flowers make an impression with colors of yellow, orange and green. It grows quickly and forms a stately pyramidical form. It also is quite long-lived, with some specimens at former presidential residences such as well-known Mount Vernon and Monticello hundreds of years old.

YELLOW AND ORANGE FLOWERS; 70 TO 90 FEET TALL; ZONES 4 TO 9

American yellowwood

CLADRASTIS KENTUKEA

With a spectacular late-spring display of pendulous panicles of fragrant white flowers, smooth gray bark and a broad, rounded crown, this is a striking focal tree. It's named for the

Tulip poplar trees grow quickly.

Desert willow trees are heat tolerant.

Western soapberry

bright yellow hue of its freshly cut wood.
WHITE FLOWERS; 30 TO 50 FEET TALL; ZONES 4 TO 8

Carolina silverbell
HALESIA CAROLINA OR TETRAPTERA
This tree rings in the spring season with silvery-white, bell-shaped flowers that dangle in pretty clusters. As its name suggests, the silverbell thrives in its native Southeast, especially along waterways. In cool, moist and well-drained conditions, it's a long-lived and easy-care tree.
WHITE FLOWERS; 30 TO 40 FEET TALL; ZONES 5 TO 8

White fringe tree
CHIONANTHUS VIRGINICUS
The large, loose panicles of fringe tree emerge in late spring and look like fluffy clouds dotting the tree's branches. Its botanical name is derived from the Greek words *chion* for snow and *anthos* for flower. This tree tolerates urban environments well and has an open, spreading habit and multiple trunks.
WHITE FLOWERS; 12 TO 20 FEET TALL; ZONES 4 TO 9

Western soapberry
SAPINDUS DRUMMONDII
Yellowish-white flowers in relaxed panicles emerge in late spring, followed by yellow-orange berries. Native to Texas, it is adaptable to varied soil conditions and grows to be equally tall and wide. The berries can get messy, and when crushed in water, they create suds.
YELLOW-WHITE FLOWERS; 25 TO 30 FEET TALL; ZONES 6 TO 9

Common sassafras
SASSAFRAS ALBIDUM
Though often recognized for its leaves—which can be three-lobed—single or mitten-shaped, this tree's flowers are just as distinctive. Yellow bunches of delicate flowers unfurl on a tree that grows into a handsome rounded canopy. As a bonus, it has vibrant fall color.
YELLOW FLOWERS; 30 TO 60 FEET TALL; ZONES 4 TO 9

Flowering Statements
Although many states selected evergreens as their state symbols, flowering trees are well-represented among the ranks of official icons.

Arizona: palo verde

Delaware: American holly

Florida and South Carolina: cabbage palmetto

Hawaii: candlenut tree

Indiana, Kentucky and Tennessee: tulip poplar

Kansas and Nebraska: eastern cottonwood

Mississippi: magnolia

Missouri and Virginia: flowering dogwood

Ohio: Ohio buckeye

Oklahoma: eastern redbud

Wyoming: plains cottonwood

Blooming Bird Magnet
An orchard oriole perches on Carolina silverbell.

Become a Pruning Pro

Get the job done right with advice from an experienced gardener.

By Niki Jabbour

FOR MOST DECIDUOUS TREES and shrubs, winter is the best time for pruning. Plants are dormant and bare, so it's easier to see the branching structure and get a sense of what needs to be removed. It's also better for the plant because winter pruning promotes quick regrowth in spring and limits the exposure of the wound to insects and disease.

The first rule of pruning is this: Don't prune unless you have a good reason. One reason could be the appearance. You might have a young plant, such as a fruit tree, and want to train it into an open canopy and balanced shape. Or maybe you want to control the size of a shrub to ensure it doesn't outgrow its space. A major reason for pruning is to encourage flowering or increase fruit production, especially in plants such as forsythia and highbush blueberry. Finally, dead, broken or hanging branches are a safety hazard, so it's best to get them out of the way.

Pruning can be an intimidating task for a lot of gardeners, but pruning mistakes are similar to a bad haircut: It may look funny for a while, but it'll grow back. Here are some tips to help you tackle winter pruning.

What to prune in winter

- Summer-flowering shrubs and trees such as rose of Sharon, crape myrtle, potentilla, smoke bush, butterfly bush and beautyberry. They produce flower buds on new growth and respond well to dormant pruning in winter. Shrubs grown for foliage, such as barberry, privet and burning bush, are also good candidates for winter pruning.
- Deciduous fruit trees such as apples, pears, cherries and plums. Dormant pruning removes some of the flower buds, but it also opens up the tree to more light and air, boosting tree health and fruit size and quality.
- Fruiting shrubs such as highbush blueberries, currants and gooseberries. Remove the oldest stems at ground level to encourage fresh fruiting branches.
- Deciduous trees such as oak, honey locust and linden. As with smaller shrubs and trees, it's easier to see the framework of the branches in the winter.

What not to prune in winter

- Spring-flowering shrubs and trees such as forsythia, lilac, quince, bigleaf hydrangea, rhododendron and azalea, which form their flower buds on wood from the previous year. These are best pruned after flowering in spring.
- Trees with winter sap flow, such as maples, birches and dogwoods. Sap loss won't hurt the trees, but it can make a mess on nearby structures. These trees are easier to prune in midsummer when sap flow isn't a problem.
- Most conifers should be pruned during their growth spurt in late spring. Do research on specific conifers for tips.

Do's

- **DO** pick a dry, sunny day, which is more comfortable for you and beneficial for the plant. Wet plants can spread disease.

- **DO** start with clean, sharp tools. If you remove diseased tissue, wipe your pruning tools with a 10% bleach solution between cuts.

- **DO** study the shape of the plant and consider each cut before you prune.

- **DO** start by removing the three D's—dead, damaged or diseased wood.

- **DO** take out any crossing branches. Rubbing injures plant tissue and invites disease. Typically, the smaller of the two competing branches is removed.

- **DO** remove water sprouts and suckers. Suckers grow from the base of the trunk or the roots of trees, while water sprouts emerge from branches. Both are vigorous, fast-growing shoots, but interfere with healthy growth, flowering and fruiting. Water sprouts on fruit trees also block air and sunlight, reducing fruiting and increasing the risk of wounds and disease.

- **DO** trim long, unbranched stems back to a healthy, outward-facing bud. This is called heading and will stimulate nearby side buds and branches to grow.

- **DO** prune overgrown or bushy trees and shrubs by making thinning cuts, the most common type of cut. This will allow more light and air to reach the center of the plant. To thin, prune the branch or stem back to its point of origin at the base of the plant, a main stem or the trunk.

- **DO** take frequent breaks to step back and study the plant to make sure your pruning looks balanced and natural.

Rose Wrangling

Pruning climbing roses encourages healthy growth, blooms for future seasons and a neat shape.

Prune and Shape

To keep vining plants such as this climbing hydrangea looking great, use pole pruners for hard-to-reach spaces.

Tough Trees

Flowering dogwoods and other trees require a pruning saw to manage branches that are too large for hand pruners or loppers.

Don'ts

- **DON'T** leave unsightly stubs, which can become diseased or infested with insects. Instead, prune to a healthy outward-facing bud or a branch.

- **DON'T** shear shrubs into unnatural shapes unless you wish to create a formal hedge or topiary. Trees and shrubs almost always look best when allowed to grow to their natural shape and size.

- **DON'T** overprune. A rule of thumb is to remove no more than a fourth to a third of the canopy per year.

- **DON'T** be shy about pruning mature neglected shrubs. Multistemmed shrubs such as lilacs, forsythias and dogwoods can be rejuvenated with the gradual removal of old wood. Begin by pruning a fourth to a third of the old stems. Repeat each year until all the old wood is removed.

- **DON'T** cut tree limbs flush to the trunk. Instead, cut the branch where it meets the branch collar. This will promote quick and healthy callusing of the wound, and it will have no need for pruning paint.

- **DON'T** forget safety! Wear eye protection. Never prune plants close to power lines or try to remove branches that can't be reached with a pole pruner. Instead, call the experts!

CHAPTER 6

Control Invaders & Prevent Disease

Maintain a healthy garden and landscape by deterring destructive visitors and common ailments while encouraging the "good guys." Our experts tell you how!

Q Toadstools are growing in the open soil and under plant leaves in my flower bed. The soil isn't too damp, so I don't know why these intruders are showing up. I pull them out and dispose of them, but they reappear. How do I get rid of them?

Dorothy Clark CULVER, OREGON

Melinda: Toadstools are the fruiting body of fungi. The underground portion of the fungus feeds on decaying wood, like old tree roots, a stump (as you see above) or lumber accidentally buried during construction. Once the fungi have decomposed the wood, their food source is gone and the mushrooms will disappear. Rake to break up or remove the toadstools if you're worried about kids or pets eating them. Otherwise, wait for drier weather and watch them disappear until the next rainy spell.

Q I lost a hedgerow of ash trees to ash borer. I was going to replace with osage orange trees, but do you have any other hardwood recommendations?

Lynn Taylor SAGINAW, MICHIGAN

Melinda: Consider using a mix of trees. Creating diverse plantings reduces the risk of an insect or disease destroying all of the plants. Osage orange trees are durable beauties, but they do produce grapefruit-size fruit when mature. Hackberry grows 40 to 60 feet tall, has a vaselike habit and yellow fall color. A variety of maples, including Miyabe and trident, have interesting bark and fall color. Turkish filbert tolerates drought, has an attractive pyramidal shape and produces edible fruit once it's mature. Male clones (branch cuttings) of Amur cork trees, such as His Majesty, Macho and Shademaster, are adaptable, have corky bark and yellow-bronze fall color, and do not produce messy fruit.

Q Is there a way to control the cabbageworms on my vegetables without affecting the caterpillars and butterflies I'm trying to attract?

Paula Anderson BEMIDJI, MINNESOTA

Melinda: Carefully cover susceptible transplants and seeds with a lightweight floating row cover at planting. These fabrics allow air, light and water through but prevent the adult cabbageworm moth from laying its eggs on your plants. The cover also protects seedlings from hungry birds and rabbits.

Q How do I control an abundance of grasshoppers in my garden?

Marge Berger NECEDAH, WISCONSIN

Melinda: Mobile grasshoppers are difficult to control. They lay their eggs in relatively dry, undisturbed sites and remain in this stage over winter. As they hatch, they move into gardens and fields where they feed on plants. Very dry winters and springs, as well as cold wet weather, reduce populations. But the insecticides labeled for the job also kill other insects, both beneficial and harmful ones. Semaspore bait is an organic control option. The active ingredient, *Nosema locustae*, is a naturally occurring single-cell protozoan that kills developing grasshoppers as well as mole, Mormon and field crickets. Apply around the garden you are trying to protect, following the instructions on the label, and sprinkle in and around the area to control these pests. Young grasshoppers eat the bait and eventually die.

Q Every year I plant daffodils and tulips. Before the ground freezes, something digs them up and leaves the bulbs near the hole. What can I do?

Caroline Hatley BARNSTEAD, NEW HAMPSHIRE

Melinda: Most animals leave daffodils alone. Try planting them away from crocus, tulips and other critter favorites to prevent accidental digging. Some gardeners have success treating the bulbs with commercial or homemade repellents before putting them in the ground. Or you can physically protect tulips and daffodils with a flower bulb cage. Place the bulbs in the cage, plant at the proper depth, then cover the bulbs and cage with soil. Another solution: Make your own barrier. Dig a hole for planting, set bulbs in place and cover with an inch or two of soil. Lay chicken wire over the top and sides of the bulb planting, then fill the remainder of the hole with soil.

Q How do you discourage whiteflies from visiting indoor houseplants?

Juli Seyfried CINCINNATI, OHIO

Melinda: Whiteflies move indoors on newly purchased plants or on houseplants that spent the summer outdoors. These pests thrive in warm, less humid winter conditions inside. Their feeding can weaken an already stressed plant but usually won't kill it. Yellow sticky traps help manage, but won't eliminate, whiteflies. Be sure to use sticky traps inside only, as they can catch small wildlife. Repeat applications of insecticides labeled for whitefly control can further manage this pest. Always be sure to read the label carefully before using a product on a plant.

Q I have mealybugs on my 20-year-old ponytail palms. Is there any way to save the plants?

Deborah McCullough
MYRTLE BEACH, SOUTH CAROLINA

Melinda: Mealybugs are a soft scale and, like all scales, can be challenging to control. Their waxy white covering protects them from most pesticides. Touch each insect with a cotton swab dipped in alcohol to dissolve this protective coat and kill the insect beneath. Insecticidal soap will kill immature, translucent mealybugs before they form their cottony covering. Try store-bought, organic lightweight horticulture oils like Summit Year-Round® Spray Oil that kill all stages of this pest with several applications. Another option includes using a systemic insecticide that is applied to the soil and absorbed by the plant. I choose not to use this for the safety of my curious grandkids and plant-eating cats.

Q What can one do to keep grackles from bird feeders? In two days they have mine empty, and I'd like to have other birds use it as well.

Paul Marsteller
ALEXANDRIA, PENNSYLVANIA

Kenn and Kimberly: If you're dealing with a large flock of grackles, the good news is that it's probably a migratory flock that will stay only a few days before moving on. If they linger too long, you might simply stop filling the feeders for a few days until they go. Or switch to a different type of feeder: a tube feeder for thistle (nyjer) seed, with very small perches, will be challenging for grackles but just fine for small finches.

Did You Know?
With careful pruning, plants like sweet-smelling wisteria can be grown as a vine, shrub or small tree.

Q For the first time last year, my beautiful 6-year-old wisteria had tons of blooms! Is it possible to keep the birds from eating the blossoms so I can enjoy them, too?

Carmen Fraser BROOKLIN, ONTARIO

Melinda: Congratulations! Your patience with wisteria paid off. Netting is cumbersome and unattractive, but usually an effective method of protecting the blooms. Or try scare tactics like placing pinwheels, clanging pans, old DVDs or small mirrors in and near the plant. You'll get the best results if you install protection before the birds visit and vary the type and location of the scare tactics you decide to use.

Q Needle cast disease has been rampant in my area, and my evergreen trees are suffering. Is there an easy-to-use and environmentally friendly cure?

Craig Voigt
NEW ROCKFORD, NORTH DAKOTA

Melinda: Needle cast is usually not deadly, but it certainly ruins the beauty and the screening value the trees provide. Fungicides that contain copper are effective against it, and some formulations are considered organic. Check the label and make sure the product is specifically labeled for controlling needle cast and that it's natural or organic. Fungicides labeled for controlling this disease can be applied when new needles are about half expanded and again three weeks later. Thorough coverage and proper timing are critical.

Also, promptly removing and destroying infected branches will help slow the spread of needle cast. Disinfect your tools with one part bleach and nine parts water—or a 70% alcohol solution—between cuts. Mulch the soil, make sure the trees get enough water during dry periods, and give them plenty of room for light and air to reach all parts of the plant.

Q For the past few years, my tomatoes have had a hard white core and been tasteless, but they were fine in the years before that. It doesn't seem to matter what variety I use or if I add compost to the soil. What can I do to grow tasty tomatoes again?

Jodi Luciano BROOKLYN, NEW YORK

Melinda: This disorder is known as internal white tissue. It's a response to environmental conditions, not to a disease or insect pest. The fruit usually looks fine on the outside, but once you cut into it, you uncover a hard white or green center. High temperatures during ripening are thought to trigger this growth. I could not find a list of the tomato varieties that are more resistant than others. My best suggestion is to keep trying new varieties, monitor the temperature and make notes on which ones perform well. Avoid or plant fewer of the varieties that experience problems with white tissue and other disorders.

Q I found a white substance at the bottom of my red tip (*Photinia*) plant. It looked like foamy soap suds or mushy snow. After several hours, it disappeared. What was it?

Nick Nicholson WILLIAMSTON, NORTH CAROLINA

Melinda: Sounds like spittlebugs, also known as froghoppers, were feeding on your red tip. These small insects hide in the substance you saw and suck plant juices. They create the foamy froth by secreting a clear, sugary substance and using their legs as billows. The froth protects the insects from predators and the environment. Control is usually not needed, especially when the populations are small. A strong blast of water is usually enough to dislodge the froth-covered insects and minimize plant damage.

Q Bermuda grass invaded my asparagus bed. What's the best way to weed without damaging the delicate root system?

Nathan Lembke
BENTONVILLE, ARKANSAS

Melinda: Removing the weeds by hand is the safest method. You can paint the unwanted grass blades with a total vegetation killer labeled for use in food gardens. Be sure the weedkiller or the weeds you just treated do not touch your asparagus plant or the emerging stems. Mulch your garden with shredded leaves, evergreen needles or other organic materials to help prevent the seeds of this and other weeds from sprouting.

Q When I bring plants in for the winter, should I be concerned that bugs are coming in, too?

Kathy McLaughlin
CENTENNIAL, COLORADO

Melinda: It's true that insects often hitch a ride indoors on plants summered outdoors. Give your plants a shower before moving them inside. A strong blast of water can dislodge many insects from the leaves and stems. Quarantine the plants for several weeks to prevent insects from spreading to your other houseplants. Replacing the soil may be more stressful on the plants than the insects and will not totally solve the problem. Organic products like horticulture oil and soap can be used to control many pests. Always read and follow label directions carefully. You don't want to harm the plants you're treating or any children and pets that may nibble on the leaves of treated plants.

Q What's the most humane way to discourage squirrels from feasting at our bird feeders?

Donna Lenfest OKEECHOBEE, FLORIDA

Melinda: This is a classic problem because squirrels eat the same things that birds love. The best approach is to keep these animals off the feeders. If a feeder is on a pole in the open and away from trees, a metal baffle on the pole will stop them from climbing up to it. On a hanging feeder, it may be possible to place a baffle above it. A wire mesh cage surrounding a feeder could allow small birds in while keeping squirrels (and larger birds) out. Some feeders are also designed to close under the weight of something as heavy as a squirrel. A local bird-feeding specialty store should be able to advise you on solutions for your yard.

Q Gambel's quail keep eating my flowers. I have tried various kinds of netting, but the quail just push through and eat everything. Can you suggest a solution?

Barbie Slavkin MESA, ARIZONA

Kenn and Kimberly: Our first thought was how lucky you are to have Gambel's quail in your yard! But we can relate to the challenge of creating a habitat for wildlife and then balancing that with the need to protect garden plants and flowers. If netting has failed, you could try creating exclosures with chicken wire. Available at most farm supply stores, chicken wire is a sturdier product that might keep the quail at bay. But if exclosures fail, you may want to reconsider the plants themselves. If the quail feast on particular plants, try eliminating those flowers and planting ones less likely to appeal to hungry birds.

Q Do you have any tips for preventing squirrels from digging in my potted plants? I've tried mothballs and repellent sprays, but nothing seems to keep them away.

Mary Rumbaugh
MIDLAND, MICHIGAN

Melinda: Squirrels are persistent and often destructive pests of container plantings. They have grown accustomed to humans and have all day to find ways to overcome barriers. It will take a variety of tactics and persistence on your part to keep them away. Try treating your plants with cayenne pepper as you plant, or consider scare tactics, like motion-sensitive sprinklers and pinwheels. Cover new plantings with fine netting to allow air, light and water through but discourage digging. The squirrels may lose interest. Once plants are established, remove the covering and monitor for squirrel damage.

Q When I got out my pots from last fall, tons of little bugs with wings covered the old soil. Can I reuse the soil?

Suzanne Foote CAYUGA, NEW YORK

Melinda: In general it's best not to save and reuse potting mix when the soil or plants are infested with insects or infected with disease. So discard that soil and clean the pots before you use them again. Dip each pot in a solution of one part bleach to nine parts water. Then rinse in clear water and they'll be ready for fresh soil and new plants!

Q. For three years my pink dogwood produced leaves in the spring, and by the end of each June, the leaves turned brown and crispy. I don't want to dig it up and throw it away. Any advice?

Theresa Safarino MADISON, ALABAMA

Melinda: Start by reviewing your watering practices. Too much, too frequent or insufficient watering causes leaves to brown and drop. Make sure the rootball and surrounding soil are watered thoroughly when the top 4 to 6 inches are crumbly and moist. Adjust watering as needed. If this doesn't fix the problem, take a close look at the leaves when they start browning. Several leaf-spot diseases cause spots to develop and may result in leaf drop. Fall cleanup and dry spring weather are usually sufficient to control these diseases. Dogwood anthracnose is a serious fungal disease affecting flowering dogwood. Brown spots with purple edges are the first to appear. The spots enlarge and eventually kill the whole leaf. Get a proper diagnosis from the local extension service or a certified arborist before you start any disease treatment.

Q. I removed a hummingbird vine, and since then, I've had suckers showing up everywhere. I've tried everything, including digging them all up. How can I get rid of them once and for all?

Jean Conger GARLAND, UTAH

Melinda: Though a real hummingbird magnet, the suckering characteristic is a big downside of this vine. Also known as trumpet vine (*Campsis radicans*), it sends up runners that can be challenging to manage. Continually pruning the shoots to the ground as they appear will eventually starve the plant, but you must remove every one. As you discovered, it can take a lot of time and effort. Another option is you can paint the leaves with a total vegetation killer. If you do, be careful not to touch nearby desirable plants and know that repeat applications will be needed. As always, be sure to read and follow label directions.

Did You Know?
Red-wings are short-distance migrants and visit feeders frequently during migration when they need the extra nutrition.

Q Red-winged blackbirds swoop in, clean out my feeders and scare other birds away. Do you have advice for keeping these pesky birds away?

Judy Green
HOUGHTON LAKE, MICHIGAN

Kenn and Kimberly: Flocks of red-wings can be disconcerting when they swarm feeders. In early spring and late fall, when they're just passing through, they may move on if you empty the feeders for a day. But if red-wings nest in marshes near you during the summer, you may not be able to keep them away. You might try using narrow tube-style seed feeders with very small perches, and sugar water feeders with no perches at all. Or you may be able to bribe the hungry red-wings to stay in one part of the yard with an open, flat feeder filled with cracked corn or other cheap feed.

Armored Visitors

Cold is an enemy of armadillos, so they primarily live in temperate, humid and warm habitats in the South.

Q How do I discourage armadillos from digging in my garden? I treated the lawn with milky spore a couple of years ago to control the grubs, but the armadillos came back with a vengeance.

Jan Brandenburg
HANCEVILLE, ALABAMA

Melinda: Armadillos eat a variety of insects, earthworms, spiders and scorpions, as well as fruits and vegetables. Managing one of their favorite insects, Japanese beetles, can help. Keep in mind it takes several years of milky spore applications to accumulate enough bacteria to effectively control the grubs. Avoid using other pesticides on the lawn and tolerate some grub damage during this time. This organic grub control primarily kills the larvae of Japanese beetles but not other insects. You may want to try using an armadillo repellent as well.

Backyard Tip
Pull purple loosestrife
out by the roots and wrap
it in a plastic garbage
bag for disposal.

Q. I replaced overgrown lawn with a mixture of natives and herbs for birds and butterflies. But now some purple loosestrife has appeared along my property line. Is there any way to get rid of it, or am I doomed to a loosestrife takeover?

Marge Berger ATHENS, WISCONSIN

Melinda: Thanks for doing your part to keep invasive plants, like purple loosestrife, out of the ecosystem. Removing these invaders as soon as you find them, before they set seed, is the best way to control small populations. Plants in your neighborhood may be providing the seeds that are infesting your plantings. Work with neighbors to rid your area of this pest. Some severely infested communities have enlisted the help of galerucella beetles, which eat purple loosestrife leaves and prevent the plant from flowering. For information, contact the Wisconsin Department of Natural Resources. Officials work with schools and citizen groups to raise, release and monitor the beetles. Those battling purple loosestrife in other states can contact their local municipality, university extension office or Department of Natural Resources for solutions.

Toads in the Garden

Learn why these amphibians are beneficial backyard guests.

By David Mizejewski

WHEN YOU THINK OF garden wildlife, it's likely that birds, butterflies and bugs come to mind first. But if so, you're missing one of the most charming of backyard creatures: toads. Not only are they cute—in a charming lumpy, bumpy sort of way—they're incredibly valuable in the garden.

Frog or Toad?

Toads are amphibians and closely related to frogs. There are about two dozen toad species in North America. Unlike aquatic frogs, toads are adapted to live in drier land environments. They have dry skin, rounded bodies, blunt noses and short legs that they walk on as often as hop. Most have tan, brown or gray coloration to blend in with soil, fallen leaves and rocks. Toads also have bumps on their skin. Contrary to myth, these aren't warts. They are called paratoid glands and they produce toxins that protect the toads from predators.

Pest Gobblers

Toads are strictly carnivorous. They feed on beetles, slugs, crickets, flies, ants and other invertebrates. Larger toad species even eat small rodents and snakes. All toads will try to eat anything they can pull into their mouths and swallow. When it comes to natural pest control, you can't do much better than a healthy toad population on your property.

Environmental Indicators

Toads, like all amphibians, are highly susceptible to environmental toxins. Their skin can readily absorb pesticides, chemical fertilizers and other pollutants. If exposed to unhealthy levels of these things, amphibians can't survive. If you have a population of toads in your yard, it's a good indication of a clean environment.

Toad sitting on garden mushrooms

Attracting Toads

Although toads don't rely on plants for food, they do benefit from them. Native plants offer habitats to natural insect populations, which are a toad's main food source. Plants also provide toads with cover to hide from predators. A bare lawn won't help attract toads, but natural garden beds filled with native plants will.

Create a brush or rock pile and leave a layer of fallen leaves to provide hiding places. Also, eliminate the use of chemical pesticides and fertilizers, which can kill toads outright and eliminate their prey.

A clean water source is also necessary. Toads lay their eggs in shallow ponds, and without water, they can't produce the next generation. In most cases, a water garden a foot or more deep will suffice. Place a small tree branch in the water, as well as aquatic vegetation, and let some leaves accumulate. Toads attach strings of their eggs to twigs and branches, and their tadpoles use the vegetation as hiding places. Start welcoming toads to your yard and enjoy the magic of listening to the trilling mating calls of male toads on warm spring nights.

3 Ways to Create a Toad Abode
Build toads a space of their own. Place your new toad home in a shady spot near a water source.

1. Half-bury a large flowerpot on its side.

2. Tip a flowerpot upside down and prop one side up with a few rocks to create an entrance.

3. Gather flat rocks and build a toad-sized house with them.

Orb-weaver
spider

The Good Bugs

From beetles to bees, discover who the "good guys" are and why you want these crawlers in your backyard.

By David Mizejewski

GOOD GARDENERS KNOW the benefits of good bugs. Most insects, spiders and the other invertebrates that get lumped together into the generic "bug" category can really be beneficial in the garden. Take a look at why you want these in your yard.

Predatory Beetles and Bugs

Among the hundreds of thousands of species in the Coleoptera (beetles) and Hemiptera (true bugs) insect orders are many predatory creatures, which dine on their plant-eating kin. Ladybird, soldier, ground and tiger beetles, along with assassin and pirate bugs, are just a few you should welcome to your garden as residents.

Bees, Wasps and Ants

All bee species are important pollinators, which are largely responsible for the seeds, nuts, berries, fruits and other plant foods that form the bottom of the food chain, feeding both the people and wildlife. So don't be so quick to shoo them away. You'll want to welcome wasps and ants as well. Avid predators, they're constantly patrolling, picking your garden clean of pests.

Caterpillars

Butterflies and moths are attractive; they're also important pollinators. Even better, their caterpillars attract birds. More than 95% of backyard birds rely on caterpillars as a primary food for their young. Attracting these insects to your garden essentially means attracting more birds.

Spiders

These arachnids are some of the most helpful garden invertebrates, but they're also among the most maligned. All spiders are predatory and feed on insects, whether they hunt using skillfully woven webs (argiope and orb-weaver spiders), by

3 Bugs You Don't Want

Mosquitoes
Not only do mosquitoes cause an itchy welt when they bite, they spread diseases. Eliminate stagnant water in your yard, where mosquitoes breed (clogged gutters are a common culprit), and wear insect repellent.

Fire Ants
These exotic ants were introduced to Alabama almost a century ago and have been proliferating ever since. They have an extremely painful sting and are displacing many native ant species. Avoid their large mounds, or call a professional exterminator to eliminate them in your yard.

Ticks
These parasitic arachnids spread diseases and are especially problematic in areas with large deer populations. Avoid areas of tall grass where ticks lie in wait. Mow pathways in your garden, wear long pants tucked in to socks, and check yourself and pets after outdoor time.

ambush (tarantulas and trapdoor spiders) or by stalking (wolf and jumping spiders).

Dragonflies and Damselflies

These aerial acrobats are a double threat. In their adult phase, they feed on all manner of flying insects, from mosquitoes to biting flies and gnats, but their aquatic larvae are no slouches, either, devouring the larvae of the same pests.

So what can you do to attract them? First, plant native species, which can support 60% more native insects than some of the more exotic ornamentals. Second, don't be too tidy. A natural garden design provides hiding and hibernation spots, as well as food and places to nest. Finally, stop using pesticides. This can be tough to do if you rely on them regularly, but they kill beneficial insects along with the ones you don't want. In the long run, they disrupt the natural order, making it more likely you'll have overall pest problems.

CHAPTER 7

Plant ID

From blooms that appear overnight to plants that have been
around for years, their identification takes skill and know-how.
Our experts can help when a plant has you guessing!

Q I admire these pretty yet unusual flowers every day as I walk into work. I'd love to plant them at my house. What is their name?

Katina Smith OSKALOOSA, IOWA

Melinda: This beauty is annual spider flower, also known by its botanical name, *Cleome hassleriana*. To grow your own, start plants from seed indoors six to eight weeks before the last spring frost. Or buy plants from a local garden center. Plant them in full sun to part shade. Once established, spider flower is drought tolerant. Beware of the thorns, but enjoy the birds, butterflies and hummingbirds that visit the plant. Watch for seedlings in next year's garden.

Q These wildflowers turn up every spring in a wooded area of my front yard. Can you tell me what they are?

Marion Clark MANASSAS, VIRGINIA

Melinda: This is a type of trillium. There are several native species of trilliums with mottled leaves found in southeastern United States. *Trillium sessile*, also known as toadshade, has maroon flowers that appear closed and are right above the leaves. Little Sweet Betsy (*Trillium cuneatum*) looks similar and has large, smelly flowers. Bloody Butcher (*Trillium recurvatum*) has maroon, claw-like flowers and yellow trillium (*Trillium luteum*) has yellow, lemon-scented flowers. I've included their botanical names because common names can vary from region to region. Plus, the scientific name makes it easier for you to do further research and help determine exactly what type you've got here. Good luck!

Q This cactus was my grandmother's and is more than 50 years old. Each spring it produces these huge red blooms. Do you recognize this variety?

Kathy Fincher BETHLEHEM, GEORGIA

Melinda: Your family heirloom is a red orchid cactus. Formerly classified as *Epiphyllum*, it is now botanically known as *Disocactus x hybridus*. This group of cactus is found in subtropical and tropical rainforests and is relatively easy to grow. Place the plant in a bright location and water thoroughly whenever the soil starts to dry. Allow the plants to go a bit drier in winter. Fertilize with a dilute solution of indoor or flowering plant fertilizer as needed when plants are actively growing, and then reduce or stop fertilizing in winter.

Q Can you identify this flower that appeared in my daughter's garden?

Beverly Younger CRYSTAL LAKE, ILLINOIS

Melinda: The shape and inside of the flower inspired its common name, spotted bellflower (*Campanula punctata*). Hardy in zones 4 to 8, it grows up to 2 feet tall. Grow this plant in full sun to partial shade with moist, well-drained soil. It's a summer-blooming perennial that makes a great cut flower and is a welcome addition to perennial, container or woodland gardens.

Q I found this plant in late December in Wisconsin and it's still green. What is it?

Michael King APPLETON, WISCONSIN

Melinda: Depending on the region, some gardeners prize this plant and others avoid it for its invasiveness. Known as donkey tail or myrtle spurge (*Euphorbia myrsinites*), the succulent is banned in several western states because it spreads quickly, crowding out important native plants. Hardy in Zones 4 to 8, it thrives in heat, full sun and well-draining soil. Tiny yellow star-shaped flowers appear on the tips of the branches and are surrounded by a yellow-green or green bract. It reseeds readily and can quickly take over a garden. Remove the fading flowers to prevent seeds from forming.

Q This beautiful tree blooms in early summer in northern Ontario. What is it?

Lorna Shepherd ECHO BAY, ONTARIO

Melinda: Don't let the beauty of this tree fool you. This is a black locust tree (*Robinia pseudoacacia*). It's native to the U.S., but it has escaped the landscape and is considered invasive or a noxious weed in much of the U.S. and Canada. The tree produces fragrant flowers that are followed by seed-filled pods, which help it spread so well. Unfortunately, it forms dense thickets in natural areas, crowding out other native plants. Because of this, I wouldn't recommend encouraging it or planting it in other areas.

Q I spotted a plant in my yard that I've never seen before. I had my husband mow around it so I could take a picture. Is it a weed?

Sandra Scaggs GRANITE CITY, ILLINOIS

Melinda: What a nice surprise to find grape hyacinth growing on your property. Animals usually leave these bulbs alone, but it looks like some two- or four-legged critter planted these in the grass. Some gardeners do intentionally plant these in the lawn for added spring color. Once the flowers fade you can mow high and these bulbs will return next year. Or dig them up and move them to the garden if you'd rather enjoy them there.

Q This came up in my mother's garden and we'd like to know what it is. The leaves are soft and velvety, but it has never bloomed. Can you identify it?

Bonnie Ellison THORSBY, ALABAMA

Melinda: Be grateful your mystery plant, velvetleaf, didn't flower. Each velvetleaf plant can produce up to 8,000 seeds, allowing it to quickly take over a garden. Pull the plants out before they have a chance to flower and set seed. Laying mulch in your flower beds will reduce the risk of any other seeds that found their way into the garden from sprouting.

Q This cactus bloomed for the first time in 15 years. Can you tell me what it is?

Shirley Leffert GREENWOOD, INDIANA

Melinda: Most cactuses that grow as tall, ribbed columnar stems were originally called cereus. Over time, some were moved into other groups based on flowering and fruiting similarities and differences. Those that remain in the cereus group tend to bloom at night with large white flowers, like yours, and are fragrant. Cereus cacti have stems with four to 10 ribs, large areoles (bumps where spines arise) and stout spines.

Did You Know?
Night-blooming cactuses are pollinated by moths. (The white blooms make them easier to find.)

Q I spotted this delicate flower that is kind of transparent and a very pretty blue-purple color. What could it be?

Kit Warner MULE CREEK, NEW MEXICO

Melinda: You've found native larkspur, most likely *Delphinium nuttallianum*. This particular larkspur is more common in open areas and dry conditions. There are several other very similar delphiniums that are distinguished by their location and more subtle features. As the blue petals pass their peak, they start to fade and develop the transparency you've captured in this photo.

Q What is this charming little plant growing on the top of my gatepost?

Madeleine Martin MOORES HILL, INDIANA

Melinda: This common lichen (*Cladonia cristatella*) is found in Canada and most of the northeastern U.S. Often called red caps or British soldiers because their tops resemble the red caps once worn by British troops, these lichens are slow-growing and are usually found on rotting wood and occasionally on the bases of healthy trees. Lichens are formed by a rare partnership between an alga or cyanobacteria and a fungus. The fungus provides the protection, while the alga or cyanobacteria bring nutrients to the party.

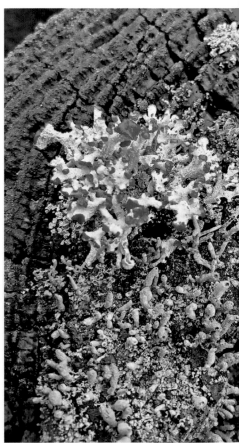

Q The blooms of this magnolia tree smell lovely in early spring and summer. Can you tell what type this is? I'd love to get another one.
Deborah Brown
BOWLING GREEN, KENTUCKY

Melinda: Your fragrant beauty looks like a sweet bay magnolia (*Magnolia virginiana*). This tree grows 10 to 20 feet tall and wide and is hardy in Zones 5 to 9. It prefers acidic soil but, unlike most magnolias, this one tolerates wet or even swampy conditions. Use it as a specimen planting, near a patio or anywhere you can enjoy the flowers and fragrance.

Patent Work
If you have a plant to share, check to see if it has a patent, which would make it illegal to propagate. Older garden plants are often safer bets for shared cuttings.

Q My sister received a cutting of this plant from a friend. What is it?

Joyce Bokina HIXSON, TENNESSEE

Melinda: Your sister is the lucky recipient of *Hibiscus mutabilis*. The seed capsules that appear after the flowers fade release fuzzy seeds, inspiring the plant's common name: cotton rose. It grows into a shrub 6 to 8 feet tall in Zones 9 though 11. In Zones 7 and 8 it may die back to the ground but reappear in spring. In colder climates it is treated as an annual or overwintered indoors. Cotton rose grows best in full sun to light shade and in rich, well-draining soil.

Q This bush has been in my family for many generations and no one seems to know its true name. We call it a "ducie" bush (we don't know how to spell it). Can you help us ID it?

Cindy Wabner SEBREE, KENTUCKY

Melinda: Your family's name for it is close. The shrub is commonly and botanically known as deutzia. It is pronounced *dut'se-a* (with a long u). This spring-flowering shrub is hardy in Zones 4 to 8 and can often grow up to 7 feet tall and wide, depending on the variety. It flowers best in full sun and tolerates most garden soil as long as it is well drained. Prune the shrub after flowering if you need to control its size and shape.

Q This plant is a mass of tiny lavender blooms from mid-August to mid-September. Bees love it! It's 3 feet high and not invasive. Do you know what it is called?

Joan Bangel EAST SYRACUSE, NEW YORK

Melinda: This heat- and salt-tolerant perennial, *Limonium latifolium*, is known by several names, including sea lavender, wide-leaf sea lavender and statice. Hardy in Zones 3 to 9, it grows best in full sun with well-drained soil. The plant can flop and might need staking when grown in heavier clay soil. Harvest a few stems to use in dried arrangements or crafts: Cut the flower stems just before the blossoms open fully, then hang upside down in a shady, airy location to dry.

Backyard Tip

Not only is sea lavender a bee favorite, butterflies love it, too.

Q I bought this tree when it was about 8 feet tall and was told it's a ponderosa tree. What is this tree really called?

Rickey Glidewell BOONEVILLE, MISSISSIPPI

Melinda: This beauty is known by several common names, including rattlebox, scarlet wisteria and false poinciana; botanically, it's called *Sesbania punicea*. Hardy in Zones 8 to 11, it prefers full sun and moist to wet soils. Bright orange flowers and attractive foliage make it easy to spot in the landscape. Unfortunately, while quite pretty, it is considered an invasive or noxious weed in many southern states and California.

Q A couple of years ago a friend gave me this plant. At one point I thought it was dead, but it bloomed! What is this plant and how should I maintain it?

Dannie Calk RIO FRIO, TEXAS

Melinda: The unusual blooms are a helpful identification clue. Your mystery plant is a celosia. Hardy in Zones 9 and 10, most of us grow this heat- and drought tolerant plant as an annual. It often reseeds, though the offspring of celosia cultivars do not always resemble the original plant. Grow celosia in full sun and water it thoroughly when the top few inches of soil start to dry. The blooms make lovely fresh and dried cut flowers.

Q This flower came up when I planted a seed mix last summer. It had beautiful, delicate foliage. What is it?
Diane Bergantz
SAN LUIS OBISPO, CALIFORNIA

Melinda: This showy annual, called spider flower or cleome, can be purchased as seeds or transplants from the garden center. The long stamens extend beyond the petals, giving the plant its spidery appearance. This favorite grows best in full sun with plenty of moisture. It is trouble-free and, once planted, usually rewards you with seedlings every year. Early season cultivation and sharing with friends are smart ways to eliminate or reduce unwanted seedlings.

Q What is this plant? I saw it on someone's porch and really like it.

Holly Harnly
MYERSTOWN, PENNSYLVANIA

Melinda: The fuzzy flowers inspired common names like chenille plant and red-hot cat's tail. Botanically known as *Acalypha hispida*, this popular houseplant is often moved outdoors for summer in full to partial shade. Keep it in bloom by removing flowers as they fade. When temperatures cool in fall, move it back indoors to a warm, sunny window. Gardeners in Zones 10 and 11 can grow chenille plants outdoors year-round, and those plants can reach 10 feet tall and 8 feet wide.

Q My aunt gave me this tree and called it something in French, but I can't find any information about it online. What is it?

Penny McPherson
ODENVILLE, ALABAMA

Melinda: That's the challenge with common names—two or more plants can share the same common name, and these names often change as they are passed along from one gardener to another. Your plant is a gardenia; its fragrant white flowers and glossy green leaves are clues to its identity. Gardenias are generally hardy outdoors in Zones 8 to 11. They thrive in sun to partial shade and moist, well-draining, acidic soils. Use an organic fertilizer or one labeled for acid-loving plants in spring. Gardeners in colder regions can grow gardenias in a container if they move the plants indoors for winter.

Q These two photos were taken the same day—one during the day and one at night. Can you tell me what this plant is and why it has a reverse blooming time?

William Goachee ROMULUS, MICHIGAN

Melinda: Your plant's common name, four-o'clocks, will help solve your mystery. As you observed, the fragrant flowers open late in the day. Four-o'clocks (*Mirabilis jalapa*) are an old-time favorite, available with red, yellow, pink, white or striped flowers. Grow four-o'clocks in sun or partial shade. They tolerate heat, pollution and just about any soil type. Hardy in Zones 9 to 11, these plants can be grown as a tender perennial there or an annual in other areas. They occasionally survive a cold winter in a sheltered location and freely reseed, so you'll have beautiful plants for years to come.

The Truth About Weeds

We'll help you figure out whether you should pull it up or let it grow.

By Melinda Myers

A No-Grow
This purple plant (purple loosestrife) might look pretty, but it's one of the most invasive weeds in North America.

Purple
loosestrife

66 **S THIS A WEED OR A FLOWER?"** I've
been in the gardening and horticulture
business for more than three decades,
and it's still one of the most common
questions I get year after year. In fact,
gardeners probably bring me a few hundred
"gifts" each spring in the form of mystery leaves,
flowers and plants.

The truth is, we've all faced this dilemma
at some point. When plants start sprouting in
spring, all those tiny leaves seem to look the same.
I don't know any gardener (myself included) who
hasn't grown a few weeds or accidentally weeded
out a few desirable plants.

So I'm here to help. Hopefully I can at least
point you in the right direction when it comes to
recognizing common backyard weeds. Doing so
will allow you to focus on your treasured garden
plants instead.

The Usual Suspects

Let's take a look at some of the most common
weeds in North America. If you can learn to
recognize these, you'll be well on your way toward
eliminating most of the unwelcome visitors in
your yard.

Teasel comes to mind right away. This
thistle look-alike, brought to North America in

Teasel

Quack grass

the 1700s for processing wool, has spread into natural spaces. Its prickly stems and leaves make it undesirable to wildlife and agriculture, so eliminate it if you find it in your yard.

Buckthorn, garlic mustard and purple loosestrife were once prized landscape plants, but they now crowd out native plants and disrupt natural ecosystems. It's definitely worth your time and energy to try to get rid of them. Their unwelcome presence reduces food sources and habitat for native birds, butterflies, beneficial insects and wildlife.

Quack grass is something most gardeners will encounter. It's easy to identify by the long, white underground rhizomes that look like roots. Any piece of the rhizome that touches the ground can start a new plant. To be successful, you must be thorough and persistent if you try to remove quack grass by hand.

Crabgrass has a smaller, more fibrous root system. It thrives in hot, dry weather, making its presence known in mid- to late summer. You'll often find it growing in gardens, short-cropped lawns and in other places subject to hot, dry conditions. Mow lawns high to help healthy lawn grass shade out the nuisance crabgrass. In the garden, you should pull crabgrass before the plants set seed, and mulch to help prevent seeds from sprouting.

5 Weeds to Reconsider

Though you may still want to manage them in the landscape, you might find that these plants, typically considered weeds, actually have value.

- Clover: Many lawn enthusiasts consider it a weed, but it's an important source of nectar for bees and a tasty treat for wildlife. Some people grow clover lawns as a more eco-friendly and low-maintenance alternative to traditional grass.

- Common purslane: This summer annual, which thrives in hot, dry conditions, is a tasty substitute for spinach. Pull it before it sets seed to keep it under control, but throw a little on your salad, too.

- Lamb's-quarters: It's moving off many weed lists and onto gourmet restaurant menus. But do a little reading before you eat: Too much can make you sick.

- Chickweed: This is another one that can quickly take over a garden, but it adds zing to a salad or sandwich.

- Dandelions: They aren't as bad as people think. Birds eat the seeds, and the leaves have long been used in early-spring salads because they're rich in vitamin C.

Clover

Nutsedge (also called nutgrass) is another common problem. The grasslike plants form underground tubers called nutlets. Persistence, early intervention and an integrated management strategy are critical for control of these weeds.

Ragweed is a plant that hay fever sufferers will particularly want to watch out for. You can usually find this pesky weed hiding behind its colorful neighbor, goldenrod. Be sure to mow it down or pull it before it has a chance to release its allergenic pollen.

Garlic mustard was brought here for medicinal purposes and food, but it has become one of the worst forest invaders. A relative of mustard, this biennial plant produces thousands of seeds that can stay in the soil for seven years or more. Pull and properly dispose of plants just before they flower.

Creeping Charlie (ground ivy) is another one I get questions about. It's easy to identify by its round, scalloped leaves, which are fragrant when crushed. This shade-tolerant plant with purple spring flowers can take over a lawn or garden bed. To get rid of it in the lawn, try a chelated iron-based weedkiller. In the garden, pull it out by hand and mulch or use a total vegetation killer.

Dame's rocket is a trickier weed, because it's often misidentified as woodland phlox, and

Creeping Charlie

it looks so pretty blooming on woodland edges in spring. Unfortunately, this nonnative weed is often included in wildflower mixes, and it quickly crowds out more desirable native plants. Look for the four-petaled flowers that distinguish this from the five-petaled flowers of phlox—and then get rid of it.

Butterfly weed

Weeds You Want

They might have "weed" in their name, but don't be fooled. You actually want these garden favorites in your backyard.

- Butterfly weed or milkweed (*ASCLEPIAS*)
- Sneezeweed (*HELENIUM*)
- Joe Pye weed (*EUTROCHIUM*, formerly *EUPATORIUM*)
- Ironweed (*VERNONIA*)
- Rosinweed (*SILPHIUM INTEGRIFOLIUM*)
- Jewelweed (*IMPATIENS CAPENSIS*)
- Soapweed (*YUCCA GLAUCA*)
- Staggerweed (*DICENTRA EXIMIA*)

Dame's rocket

Thistle is another tricky one. Birds and butterflies love it, but gardeners and farmers hate it. Many thistles are listed as noxious weeds; they can quickly infiltrate and take over the garden. To control the spread, try removing them before they flower and set seed.

Field bindweed is one of the hardest weeds to get under control. It has flowers like a morning glory, and a deep root system, which makes it drought tolerant and difficult to eliminate. Your best bet is to keep pulling the weeds as early as possible. Mulching will help prevent seeds from sprouting.

Poison ivy is the ultimate weed to avoid. "Leaves of three, let it be" is old but wise advice. All parts of poison ivy can cause an allergic reaction. You may stumble on it during a hike or find it creeping along the ground or crawling up a tree. Wear protective clothing and wash thoroughly after touching.

Of course, many other weeds can invade your garden, stealing important nutrients from the plants you value. If you happen to come across a mystery plant, take a few pictures, making sure you get photos of the leaves, flowers and the plant as a whole. Then seek out a local resource before you pull it up or let it grow. Good luck!

Poison ivy

Field bindweed

Nutsedge

Top 10 Plants for Fragrance

If you have a weakness for sweet-smelling blooms, consider adding some of these to your garden.

By Sally Roth

T**HE PLEASURE OF A GARDEN** goes deeper than its pretty face. It's honeysuckle on a warm June night. A ruffly rose you can't pass without stopping to breathe deep. A branch of apple blossoms, a sprig of lemon verbena, a carpet of chamomile—hundreds of plants tickle our sense of smell.

We've narrowed our list down to 10 supremely scented flowers. Renowned for their fragrance for centuries, they're wonderful treasures to discover anew. All are easy to grow, and every one will add another layer of delight to your garden.

Heliotrope

1. Oriental lilies

LILIUM HYBRIDS, ZONES 5 TO 10

The huge, extravagant flowers of Oriental lilies are showstoppers, and their intoxicating scent is so heavy and sweet you can almost taste it. To some noses, the fragrance is a bit much; plant in the middle or back of the bed to dilute the aroma. **Why we love it:** Just three bulbs are enough to perfume a big area. Pink Stargazer and white Casa Blanca are even more beautiful in the garden than in florist bouquets.

2. Dianthus

DIANTHUS HYBRIDS, ZONES 3 TO 9

The spicy clove scent of the flowers many refer to as "pinks" is legendary, but some pinks actually have no scent at all. Sniff before you buy, and you won't be disappointed. Bath's Pink is an old reliable bloomer with pastel pink flowers. Mrs. Sinkins, a favorite since Victorian days, has fluffy white flowers. **Why we love it:** The tight mound of gray foliage is just as appealing as the deliciously spicy flowers that bloom above it.

3. Heliotrope

HELIOTROPIUM ARBORESCENS, ZONES 10-11, ANNUAL ELSEWHERE

Grown in Europe for perfumes, heliotrope is beloved for its delicious vanilla scent, with notes of sweet almond or cherry. Its rich purple flowers are real knockouts; elegant white cultivars are available, too. **Why we love it:** With just a little deadheading to keep the flowers coming, heliotrope blooms until frost. You can pot up cuttings of flowering stems to bloom on a sunny windowsill all winter.

Oriental
lily

4. Garden phlox

PHLOX PANICULATA, P. MACULATA, ZONES 3 TO 9

Garden phlox rewards you with abundant blooms that continue for at least two months. You'll smell its sweet, slightly spicy aroma every time you walk by. To minimize mildew, thin out half of the new stems in spring for better air circulation, or try mildew-resistant Jeana, a pinky purple, or the pure white David cultivar.

Why we love it: Phlox is a backbone of the summer garden. For unusual hues, try Orange Perfection or Blue Paradise.

5. Lily-of-the-valley

CONVALLARIA MAJALIS, ZONES 3 TO 8

These dainty stems of dangling bells have a sweet, heavy scent so unique that in France it's a signature perfume called muguet. The pretty lily-of-the-valley loves shade, and it multiplies to form thick colonies. It can be aggressive, so plant it where it can be contained.

Why we love it: Simple leaves turn golden yellow in fall, accented by stems of translucent red berries. Try Rosea with pale pink blooms, as well as those with classic white flowers.

6. Common lilac

SYRINGA VULGARIS, ZONES 3 TO 7

Who can resist an armload of lilacs in May? Choose classic lilac color, or deep wine red, blue-lilac, pure white, even pink. Bloomerang® Purple reblooms through summer. Angel White needs less winter chill; it thrives to Zone 8.

Why we love it: So long-lived that it often survives even after a house is long gone, a lilac needs no coddling beyond regular watering its first year.

7. Mock orange

PHILADELPHUS CORONARIUS, ZONES 4 TO 8

Orange blossoms are blessed with a sublime fragrance, but growing citrus is possible only in

Lily-of-the-valley

Lilac

very mild areas. Meet mock orange, an old-fashioned shrub that almost passes as perfume. Be sure to get the single-flowering bloom; double-flowered mock orange (*Philadelphus x virginalis*) is only slightly scented.

Why we love it: Pristine white flowers create a perfect bower to back a garden bench. Buy this shrub in bloom—individual plants vary in the strength of their scent.

8. Woodland tulip

TULIPA SYLVESTRIS, ZONES ZONES 5 TO 9

It's a tulip, but it smells heavenly, it thrives in shade and it's relaxed, not stiffly upright. And the oddest thing of all—it spreads via underground stolons (runners) from the bulbs.

Why we love it: *Sylvestris* means "of the woods," so splash its sunshine beneath shade trees—this tulip lends itself to the natural look. Buy it from Monticello (*monticelloshop.org*), where Thomas Jefferson enjoyed it, or from bulb suppliers.

9. Sweet alyssum

LOBULARIA MARITIMA, ANNUAL

Surround yourself with the scent of warm honey by planting this native Mediterranean wildflower along walkways or in pots on the patio. Shear it back when it gets straggly in summer heat, and it'll soon come roaring back.

Why we love it: It's the ultimate fast fill-in for bare spaces. It also provides a wonderful softening effect in beds or pots. And the colors! Try a modern twist with the mouthwatering salmon, apricot and lemony hues of the exciting Aphrodite series.

Sweet alyssum

10. Sweet iris

IRIS PALLIDA

Striped Variegata is the most common form of this iris, whose purple blossoms smell just like grape soda. Rhizomes are the orris root used in many perfumes.

Why we love it: The easy-to-recognize scent, a hit with kids of all ages, is sniffable from yards away. Even when the plant's not in bloom, its bold leaves stand out like exclamation points among softer perennials.

Sweet iris

CHAPTER 8

Butterflies & Pollinators

From migration patterns to identification tips, learn more about nature's most interesting and beneficial creatures. Then create a backyard haven to welcome them!

Q I have 20 or more swallowtail butterfly caterpillars on my fennel plant. How can I help them survive the winter?

Lisa Bellando DENVILLE, NEW JERSEY

Kenn and Kimberly: Fennel is a favored host plant for caterpillars of the black swallowtail. Each caterpillar of the last fall generation will pupate before winter sets in, climbing up a vertical stick before transforming into a chrysalis. They'll overwinter in that stage, emerging as adults in spring. If you want to protect them from predators, you could put an enclosure around them or bring them into a screened-in porch, but don't bring them into a warm, lighted house. They will need the intense cold and the short daylight hours of a natural winter. If they're indoors, the adults might emerge in midwinter, when they couldn't survive outside.

Q One fall, I found this dried maple leaf with a cocoon inside still attached to a branch. The cocoon was about half an inch wide and 2 inches long. Sometime during the spring, it disappeared. What do you think was inside?

Karen Webster CADILLAC, MICHIGAN

Kenn and Kimberly: This is the cocoon of a wild silk moth species, almost certainly a polyphemus moth. The polyphemus is one of the largest and most beautiful moths in North America, and maples are among the favored host plants for their stout green caterpillars. The showy adults live for only a few days, just long enough to mate and lay eggs. If you're lucky, you might spot one in late spring or early summer.

Q I raised black swallowtails this year. Seven caterpillars have remained chrysalises. How do I store them so that they become butterflies in the spring?

Teresa Savage CANTON, MICHIGAN

Kenn and Kimberly: It's normal for a black swallowtail to spend the winter in the chrysalis stage, then emerge as an adult in spring. The chrysalis contains chemicals that act as antifreeze so it can survive cold temperatures. It's best to keep it in outdoorsy conditions, not in a warm house. We recommend someplace like an unheated garage or a screened-in porch. Place the chrysalis inside a container that protects it from mice or other animals, with ventilation for free airflow. The container should be large enough that the adult has room to spread its wings when it emerges.

Q This common buckeye has "common" in its name, but I don't often see them in my area. Are they more widespread in other areas of the U.S.?

Lynn Craska
BEACON FALLS, CONNECTICUT

Kenn and Kimberly: The "common" part of this butterfly's name is to distinguish it from other species, such as mangrove buckeyes and tropical buckeyes, that live in the American tropics. Common buckeyes can be quite numerous in southern states. They move northward in summer, and sometimes show up in strong numbers as far north as New England and the Great Lakes. But in most years, they are uncommon in your part of Connecticut.

Q At dusk I noticed bumblebees that appeared to be sleeping on my purple coneflowers. They didn't stir even when I came close. Do bees sleep?

LeAnn Coberly CINCINNATI, OHIO

Kenn and Kimberly: Yes, you might see bees catching a few Z's. Like other insects, they enter a resting phase that's somewhat similar to the kind of sleep that we experience. Bumblebees, in particular, often rest overnight on flowers—especially lavender or members of the aster family, like coneflowers, cosmos and sunflowers. The ones you saw were more likely to be males, since the females usually go back to the nest at night.

Q I saw this monarch feeding in my backyard in October and wondered where it might be headed. Do monarchs migrate this late?

Joanne Pinsonneault CHATHAM, ONTARIO

Kenn and Kimberly: The great monarch migration is an amazing phenomenon. The monarchs that hatch in your area of eastern Canada in early fall are the great-great-grandchildren of those that spent the winter in Mexico and migrated north in spring. Somehow these hatched monarchs know they need to fly south again. In southern Ontario, large numbers of monarchs migrate through Point Pelee National Park in fall. Peak monarch flight is usually in September, but some continue through mid-October, so you saw one of the late ones.

Milkweed Matters

Monarchs need milkweed to survive because the plant plays host to monarch eggs and caterpillars. Luckily, milkweed is easy for gardeners to grow, and with more than 100 varieties to choose from, there are plenty of options native to your area.

Q Does milkweed grow back or do I have to replant it every year?

Annette Henry McKEESPORT, PENNSYLVANIA

Melinda: Common milkweed is a perennial that's hardy in your area and throughout Zones 3 to 8. Watch for plants to emerge this spring. Once established and flowering, plants spread by underground rhizomes (horizontal stems) and scattered seeds. Milkweed thrives in well-draining soil but struggles in overly wet and poorly draining areas. Although it's drought-tolerant, it needs sufficient water for the first two years.

Grow Local

Use *plantnative.org* to find out which varieties of milkweed are native to your area and where you can buy them.

Q What type of dragonfly is this? It frequents our backyard, and we've never seen a red dragonfly.

Chris Fisher
VANCOUVER, WASHINGTON

Kenn and Kimberly: You're right, red is not a common color for dragonflies. This beauty is called a flame skimmer, and you're lucky to have it in your yard—although flame skimmers are common in some parts of the West, they enter the state of Washington only in your area, just north of the Oregon border. Some smaller types of red dragonflies, called meadowhawks, are more widespread, so you might see those elsewhere in Washington.

Q. My area was affected by wildfires in fall. The next spring, thousands of painted ladies migrated through. Are the events related?

Hilary Calce
THOUSAND OAKS, CALIFORNIA

Kenn and Kimberly: These massive movements of painted lady butterflies happen only occasionally, but they can be spectacular. They're not as predictable as the migration of monarch butterflies, though. The painted ladies build up huge populations and then stage these massive flights only when the rains have been exactly right for growth of the plants their caterpillars eat—in this case, probably a variety of annuals coming up in late winter. It's possible that many of these plants came up in the areas that had burned in the fall, but the timing also could be just a coincidence.

Get Growing
This Inspired Violet butterfly bush is a seedless noninvasive that attracts bees, butterflies and hummingbirds.

Q I can't seem to find information about growing butterfly bushes in containers. How do they fare, and is it worth trying?

Emily Rumpf CATO, NEW YORK

Melinda: Butterfly bushes, as well as other trees, shrubs and perennials, can be grown in containers. You'll have the greatest chance at winter survival growing plants that are at least one zone hardier than your region. In cold climates, you will need to provide extra winter protection. Move the plants into an unheated garage and water any time the soil is thawed and dry. Or cover the roots with wood chips and surround with bagged soil or some other type of insulation. Another option is to sink the pot in a vacant part of your garden that is sheltered.

Q. Where do the black swallowtail caterpillars on my dill plants spend their winter?

Vicki Brown OMAHA, NEBRASKA

Kenn and Kimberly: We applaud you for sharing your dill with the caterpillars. It's wonderful to watch the life cycle of butterflies—and host plants are a vital part of the process. It seems hard to believe that something so small and delicate could survive the winter, but the last generation of black swallowtails from late summer or fall will overwinter in the chrysalis stage, emerging as adults in spring. The chrysalis, looking a little like a rolled-up leaf, is usually attached to a vertical stem of a plant.

Q. I came across a group of these butterflies in October. Shouldn't they be heading south?

Susan Higbie GROSSE POINTE FARMS, MICHIGAN

Kenn and Kimberly: You've witnessed a fascinating phenomenon—the migration of painted lady butterflies. They're not common in Michigan and the Upper Midwest, but once every few years they suddenly show up in big numbers. This typically happens in summer or fall. The monarch butterflies that migrate through Michigan in autumn are headed south to the mountains of Mexico, but painted lady butterflies don't have such a definite destination, and they may be migrating in any direction.

Q I have two large butterfly bushes and no butterflies. There are petunias nearby—do some plants repel butterflies?

Dawn Corbin HOP BOTTOM, PENNSYLVANIA

Melinda: Both petunias and butterfly bushes are butterfly favorites. I've found that the number of winged visitors to my plantings varies from year to year, depending on the previous winter, wind patterns and other environmental factors. If this is a yearly problem, consider placing a flat stone in a sunny spot in the garden for butterflies to warm up and recharge. Sink a bucket of damp sand in the garden and add a pinch of sea salt or wood ash. This provides a gathering place for butterflies to lap up some needed minerals.

Eastern tiger swallowtail on butterfly bush

Q How can I keep wasps away from the caterpillars I raise?

Margie Sloane OVIEDO, FLORIDA

Kenn and Kimberly: When we're raising caterpillars, it's sad to see them killed by parasites or eaten by predators, and it doesn't help to know that this is a normal thing. If every one of the hundreds of eggs laid by female monarchs were to hatch and survive to adulthood, we'd soon be knee-deep in butterflies. It's possible to bring caterpillars indoors and raise them in a cage or terrarium, but there's some evidence that monarchs raised indoors may have trouble navigating in their migration. You can also put a small fine mesh enclosure around outdoor milkweed plants that are hosting caterpillars to keep most insects out. That approach requires constant monitoring, however.

Q Are butterfly houses more wishful thinking than practical?

Sue Gronholz
BEAVER DAM, WISCONSIN

Kenn and Kimberly: While most kinds of butterflies survive through the winter in the egg, caterpillar or pupa stage, a few hibernate as adults. Examples include mourning cloaks, commas, question marks and tortoiseshells. These hibernating adults usually seek out bark crevices or other sheltered spots, but they'll also use butterfly houses that feature vertical grooves cut deep into the wood. Even if they use your butterfly house, you may not see them as they slip inside sometime in fall and stay for weeks. So it's hard to gauge their effectiveness, but it doesn't hurt to put one of these shelters near your garden.

Monarch on milkweed

Q What milkweeds have long-lasting blooms and can be successfully grown in the Midwest?

Jennifer Broadstreet Hess
MARION, KANSAS

Melinda: Monarchs need milkweed plants to reproduce, and common milkweed is their favorite. Its flowers are fragrant, but the plants are very aggressive and require attention to keep them contained. Swamp milkweed, also known as red milkweed, tolerates moist to wet as well as average soils. It grows about 3 to 5 feet tall and has fragrant pink flowers in early-to-mid summer. The popular orange-flowering butterfly weed tolerates hot, dry weather and thrives in well-draining soil. It also is less aggressive than common milkweed and blooms for months! All three are native to the Midwest and are good choices for you and the monarchs.

Seeing Stripes

All monarch caterpillars have white, yellow and black bands, and one set of black filaments at either end.

Q All of the monarch caterpillars on my milkweed have suddenly disappeared. What happened to them?

Carol Lineberry CUMMING, GEORGIA

Kenn and Kimberly: There are a number of potential answers to this CSI (caterpillar scene investigation). Since they feed on toxic milkweed, monarch caterpillars don't have many predators, so it's unlikely that something ate all the caterpillars in a short time. Depending on how large the caterpillars were at the time of their disappearance, it's possible that they left the milkweed and went off to pupate—they may crawl many yards away before they climb to some overhanging support to form the chrysalis. It's also possible that they simply crawled off to find a fresh, new plant.

Q This insect doesn't quite look like a dragonfly or butterfly. Can you ID it?

Kalwant Grewal
ST. AUGUSTINE, FLORIDA

Kenn and Kimberly: This is an insect that's sure to cause a little confusion, because it's a moth that mimics a wasp. It's called the oleander moth or polka-dot wasp moth, a tropical species that's widespread in Florida. As one of its names suggests, its caterpillars eat the leaves of oleander bushes. The adults are active in the daytime, visiting a wide variety of flowers. Predators leave them alone because they look so much like wasps.

Q This butterfly visited my garden last fall. Can you identify it?

Helen Fojtik WHARTON, TEXAS

Kenn and Kimberly: What a treat to see this in your garden! It's a tropical butterfly, the Julia heliconian, sometimes called Julia longwing. In the U.S., it lives mainly in southern Texas and Florida. Ordinarily, it is recognized by its long wings and overall plain orange color. The individual you photographed is even more unusual because of those very pale patches on the wings, a rare variation on the normal color. If you grow passion vine, you might attract more Julias or other kinds of longwings because that is the food plant for their caterpillars.

Q What are these red bugs, and can they harm my butterfly weeds?

Nancy Dietrich DUNDALK, MARYLAND

Melinda: These colorful insects are milkweed bugs in their immature stage. Adults are flatter, more elongated, and orange and black, and they resemble a boxelder bug. The immature bugs feed on the plant's sap and seeds. To get at the sap, they inject a chemical into the plant tissue. This liquefies the tissue, allowing them to suck it up. They don't cause significant harm to plants, but gardeners in warmer areas, where the bugs may overwinter, can remove leaf litter and spent stalks to help reduce next year's population.

Q I collected close to 100 milkweed seedpods. How do I get them to grow? Someone told me to spread them over mulch and lightly work them in.

Steve Ripp NEENAH, WISCONSIN

Melinda: Many gardeners have found collecting and growing milkweed plants from seed a bit challenging. The seeds must be mature to sprout, so collect seeds from pods just before or as the pods split open. Increase your chance of success by removing the seeds from the pod. Separate the seed from the fluff and store in the refrigerator or an airtight container for several months. This cold treatment is needed to end dormancy and increase sprouting success. Sow seeds indoors in a quality potting or seed-starting mix. Move transplants into the garden after the danger of frost. You can also plant seeds directly outdoors in the fall.

Great spangled fritillary on milkweed

Malachite
butterfly
on tropical
milkweed

Q Are there any container annuals that butterflies will visit?

Donna Devillez
BROOKLYN, CONNECTICUT

Melinda: You'll be amazed by how many butterflies you can attract with a flower-filled planter. Pentas are a butterfly magnet and are often found in butterfly houses. If you're looking for something heat and drought tolerant, lantana is another favorite. Include some flat daisylike blossoms of single zinnias, cosmos and dahlias. Add fragrant heliotrope for both your benefit and the butterflies'. Grow cool-weather tolerant annuals, such as pansies and sweet alyssum, to provide nectar early or late in the season.

FAR RIGHT: KEVIN COLLISON/SHUTTERSTOCK

Q This flier's wings are totally transparent, and it has a wonderful pompom that sparkles on its tail. What is it?

Leoria Moore JOHNSON CITY, TEXAS

Kenn and Kimberly: Believe it or not, this beautiful sparkly creature is a moth. Its English name is melonworm moth, because its caterpillars feed on the leaves of melons, squash and related plants. Its scientific name, *Diaphania hyalinata*, seems more descriptive of the adult, since both "diaphanous" and "hyaline" refer to things that are translucent, clear or glassy. Melonworm moths are mostly tropical and subtropical, but they may wander far to the north, especially in fall.

Q This strange moth acts just like a hummingbird. What could it be?

Diana Frye OTTUMWA, IOWA

Kenn and Kimberly: Your mystery guest is a member of the sphinx moth family. More than 100 species of these big insects live in North America. Most of them feed by hovering in front of flowers, just like hummingbirds. Many sphinx moths are active only at night, zooming around gardens and meadows in the dark. The one in your photo, the white-lined sphinx, may fly by day or night. It's recognized by its striped and checkered body, white lines on the forewings, and broad pink stripe on the hindwings.

Q Do any types of native shade-tolerant plants attract butterflies?

Adrianne Long FREDERICK, MARYLAND

Melinda: You may be surprised to find a variety of native plants that tolerate shade and support butterflies. Always be sure to match the plant to the level of shade in your garden. Here are a few woodland natives to try. Start the season with Virginia bluebells, mixing them with other perennials to mask the large leaves that die back soon after flowering. Wild geraniums (*Geranium maculatum*), rose pink to lavender, appear during the cooler months in spring. Woodland phlox, with bluish flowers, appear in late spring. Foam flowers (*Tiarella cordifolia*) produce spikes of white flowers, and their foliage remains attractive all season long, even evergreen where winters are mild. Add a spark of color with the red and yellow blooms of Indian pinks, move on to the stately blooms of black cohosh (*Actaea racemosa*) and finish up the season with native turtleheads.

Eastern tiger swallowtail on woodland phlox

Plan for Latecomers

It may be easiest to see your favorite butterflies in summer, but be sure to plant some blooms that flower in autumn to support migrating fliers. Some of their favorites include sedum, asters, lantana, bluebeard and pentas.

Butterfly Basics

Take notice of the flying flowers in your backyard—they're pretty incredible!

By David Mizejewski

WATCHING BUTTERFLIES flitting about in the backyard never gets old. Yet with the hundreds of species out there, it can be hard to figure out just what's what. Experts know a few tricks, though. Think of this as your butterfly ID cheat sheet.

Look for Color, Size, Shape

Butterflies come in a variety of colors, sizes and shapes, so make a mental note of these characteristics when you spot a species you don't know. Even better, take a photo so you can look it up later.

Some butterflies have wing shapes or marks that you'll start to recognize by family. The skippers, for instance, have small wings, while the longwings have narrow wings, and the commas and question marks have "punctuation" on their wings. It's relatively easy to spot the more distinctive monarchs, swallowtails and admirals, but see if you can identify the sexes by their slightly different markings, or the variations based on region.

Location and Habitat

Region and habitat are also important identification tools. Few species are found across the entire continent; in fact, some have very limited ranges.

Type of habitat matters, too. It's easy to confuse a pipevine swallowtail with a similarly colored red-spotted purple—unless you know that the former prefers sunny fields and open woodlands and feeds on flower nectar, while the red-spotted purple lives deeper in the forest and feeds on items like fallen fruits, sap and even dung and carrion.

Butterfly vs. Moth

Here's another question to ask: Is your "butterfly" really a moth? Many moths are drably colored, but that isn't a foolproof ID because some are just as colorful as butterflies. The boldly spotted leopard moth is often mistaken for a butterfly. The sea-foam green of a luna moth and the yellow and pink of an io moth can also be confused with butterfly wings.

Here are some more reliable differences. Generally, butterflies are active during the day,

Male black swallowtail on a zinnia

LEFT: SARAH CATES/SHUTTERSTOCK; TOP RIGHT: DAVE WELLING; BOTTOM RIGHT: CAROL L. EDWARDS

Above: A white peacock butterfly sits above a male monarch, which has a black spot on each hindwing. Right: Look for the question mark butterfly near wooded areas.

while the majority of moths are nocturnal (with some striking exceptions). Moth antennae are either feathery or threadlike, while butterfly antennae are smooth and end in a small knob. Finally, butterflies fold up their delicate wings over their bodies while resting. Moths, on the other hand, usually fold their wings down alongside their bodies.

Caterpillars and Host Plants

It's important to remember that all butterflies start out life as caterpillars. Like the winged adults, species of caterpillars vary widely in appearance. Identifying the caterpillars in your garden will tell you which butterflies you can expect to see. Pay attention to which plant your caterpillar is eating. Each species can feed only upon a limited number of plants, so knowing the host plant is a big clue.

Butterfly-Friendly Backyard Beauty

Ready for a backyard butterfly haven?
Follow these simple steps to win over
your favorite fliers.

By Jill M. Staake

Great spangled
fritillary on purple
coneflower

Clouded sulphur on salvia

F YOU HAVE attracting butterflies on the brain, it's time to turn your yard into a nonstop butterfly bonanza. When it comes to butterflies, it really is as simple as, "If you build it, they will come." The best butterfly gardens take a little planning but are pretty self-sufficient once they're up and blooming. Choose the right plants for the right place, remember to provide some water and shelter, and then sit back and wait for the flutter of tiny wings!

Location, location, location

Though open sunny meadows often come to mind when people think of butterflies, don't be worried if you only have a small space. Butterfly gardening can be as small as a few pots on your back porch, or as large as your whole yard. Be sure to include some shady spots if possible, since some butterflies prefer it. Just remember that the best butterfly gardens can sometimes look a little overgrown or ragged, so don't expect to make this a formal focal point if a pristine garden is important to you.

Before you plant

All wildlife gardeners should avoid overuse of pesticides, herbicides and fertilizers that can have harmful effects. Once you've chosen a spot, begin by prepping the soil with plenty of compost so your plants will thrive without much additional fertilization. If you need to kill off grass in the area, cover it well with a layer of newspaper, cardboard or weed cloth and add about 4 inches of mulch on top.

Butterfly buffet

Most butterflies get the majority of their diet from nectar-producing plants, so these should make up the largest part of your garden. Choose native plants when possible. These will thrive with little care and often draw the most butterflies. Anchor your garden with a few larger nectar-producing shrubs and add groupings of flowering plants in a variety of colors, heights and flower sizes. Be sure to choose plants that flower in early spring as well as late fall—times when butterflies sometimes struggle to find food.

Your local extension office can provide a list of the best nectar plants for your area, but good bets for almost anyone include salvia, lantana, pentas, aster, marigold, zinnia and coneflower. Buddleia, also known as butterfly bush, can be a good choice in some areas, but check to be sure it's not considered invasive before you plant.

Not all butterflies rely on nectar plants. Some, like mourning cloaks and red-spotted purples, actually prefer to feed on tree sap or rotting fruit. You can offer fruit like bananas, strawberries and oranges for these butterflies. Keep ants away by filling a shallow dish with water and setting the fruit in the middle.

Drink up

Butterflies get most of the water they need from nectar, but not all. Butterflies use their delicate proboscises to sip water from dewdrops and

Question mark on butterfly bush

Eastern tiger swallowtail on purple coneflower

10 Most Wanted Backyard Butterflies

- Monarch
- Painted lady
- Tiger swallowtail
- Red admiral
- Giant swallowtail
- Mourning cloak
- Question mark
- Great spangled fritillary
- Clouded sulphur
- Black swallowtail

puddles. Some butterflies, like sulphurs and tiger swallowtails, are especially likely to gather in large numbers around muddy areas; the mud provides much-needed salts for them. Mimic these natural water areas with a shallow dish of wet sand or mud, or spray down your garden with a fine mist to provide tiny droplets of water on the plants.

Host plants

Any legitimate wildlife garden provides a place for creatures to raise their young. While butterflies are anything but dutiful parents—they lay their eggs and then leave the young caterpillars to fend for themselves—they do need places to deposit their eggs. Each butterfly species has a plant or group of plants that their caterpillars will eat, known as host plants. The best way to attract a wider variety of butterflies is to provide the host plants they need. Just remember that the purpose of these plants is to feed caterpillars, so the plants will get chewed up and defoliated. For once, holes in the leaves means gardeners are doing something right!

LEFT TO RIGHT: CAMILLE ORELLI/TERRY WILD STOCK, CAROL L. EDWARDS, DAVE WELLING

Giant swallowtail
on coneflower

To determine the best host plants for your garden, start by finding out which butterflies are regular visitors to your area. Once again, extension offices or local butterfly gardens are a great source of information. Then start seeking out the host plants these butterflies need. They are almost always native plants, and more often than not, they're what others might consider weeds. No good butterfly garden can do without them, though, so choose those that best suit your site and plant as many as you possibly can.

Host plants vary by area, but just about anyone can plant milkweed for monarchs, hollyhocks for painted ladies and violets for great spangled fritillaries. Some butterfly and moth caterpillars use trees, too, so if you have space, consider adding ash or willow for tiger swallowtails and mourning cloaks.

Shelter from the storm

Butterflies are small and fragile creatures. Raindrops can seem more like bowling balls to them, so when bad weather threatens, butterflies seek shelter. They also need places to roost overnight. Though you can buy ready-made wooden butterfly houses, you'll find butterflies are more likely to use natural areas like tall grasses and thick shrubs. Some butterflies even overwinter in crevices in tree bark and rocks. Others spend the winter as caterpillars or chrysalides buried deep in the leaf litter beneath trees, so don't be too quick to remove all that fallen foliage each autumn.

Sit back, relax and be sure to enjoy the show

To get the most out of your butterfly garden, observe the space at different times of day. In the morning, butterflies are a little slow to get started, especially if the air is cooler, so it's a wonderful time to take photos. Sunny afternoons bring out butterflies in high numbers, and the evenings are the time to enjoy beautiful moths. Take time to hunt for caterpillars, too, and buy a good field guide to learn what to look for. Most of all, find a little time each day to sit quietly and watch your winged visitors come and go. It makes all the planning and preparation worth the effort!

CHAPTER 9

Unusual Sightings

Strange-looking winged visitors? Peculiar plants? Nature has a way of keeping us guessing. Our experts are here to solve some of the biggest backyard mysteries.

Q One winter this northern bobwhite sat on our back fence for more than an hour and allowed my wife, Amy, to get close enough to take photos. Bobwhites are not supposed to be in southern Idaho, so what was it doing in our yard?

Eric Adams MERIDIAN, IDAHO

Kenn and Kimberly: You're right, northern bobwhites aren't native to anyplace near Idaho, although there are a few small introduced populations in the Pacific Northwest. Bobwhites are often raised in captivity; sportsmen's groups sometimes release them into the wild, or use them to train hunting dogs how to "point" at game. Because the one in your yard acted so tame, it was probably one of these pen-raised and released birds.

Q One year, my healthy black-eyed Susans looked like this. They were normal the next year. What's going on?

Ann Dahlke BELLA VISTA, ARKANSAS

Melinda: This is a common occurrence with black-eyed Susans, lilies, some cactuses and other plants. It is a disorder called fasciation that may result from insects feeding, mechanical injury, genetics or some unknown cause. The abnormal growth may occur on the stem, flower, fruit or roots and may be flattened, crested or contorted. There is usually no need to be concerned. Enjoy the smiling blossom or remove it if you don't like the look.

Q On a recent outing to Horicon Marsh in Wisconsin, I photographed this bird among some Canada geese. What kind is it?

Lynette Redner DELAVAN, WISCONSIN

Kenn and Kimberly: Snow geese come in two color morphs: one white with black wingtips, the other blue-gray with a white head, often called "blue goose." At a glance, this looks like it could be the latter. But a couple of things about it seem odd, like the mostly black bill—on an adult snow goose the bill should be mostly pink. Being with Canada geese is also suspicious, because snow geese usually travel in flocks of their own. Size might be the key: If it was a lot smaller than the Canada geese, it was probably an odd snow goose. If it was close to their size, it may have been a hybrid.

Q I pulled out my Blackie sweet potato vine and found two potatoes that had been growing under the soil. Are these edible?

Kelly Bruno FRAMINGHAM, MASSACHUSETTS

Melinda: The ornamental sweet potato vines are cultivars of the edible sweet potato. The tuberous roots of these ornamental sweet potato vines are edible, though most gardeners say the flavor is not as good as those grown in vegetable gardens. Some gardeners store the tuberous roots over winter and plant them in the garden or a container in spring. However, the results are usually not as uniform or as attractive as starting with new plants or cuttings.

Q Why did an extra row of green petals grow around this yellow bloom? Another flower on the same stem looked completely normal.

John and Judy Hayhicz MONROEVILLE, NEW JERSEY

Melinda: Aster yellows likely caused this bizarre growth. This phytoplasma disease organism could have been carried from infected plants to healthy specimens by an aster yellow leafhopper. This disease can attack more than 300 types of plants, such as rudbeckias, coneflowers and marigolds, or a variety of vegetables, including lettuce, celery and carrots. Infected plants often survive, but they serve as a source for future infections. Remove infected plants to reduce the source of disease that can be transmitted to your healthy plants.

Q This bird seems to be a house finch, but we've never heard of a dark morph. What is it?
James and Roxie Lofton
PORTALES, NEW MEXICO

Kenn and Kimberly: This variation is very rare: a house finch with melanistic feathers. Birds are sometimes leucistic, a condition with which they lack some or all of the melanin pigment in their feathers. The opposite, an excessive amount of melanin, seems to occur far less often. The blackness of the wing and tail feathers here is exceptional and made us wonder if the bird might have been stained by oil or something similar, especially since the edges of the feathers look ragged. But the evenly dark color of many of the other feathers suggests we're seeing a pigment issue rather than staining.

Did You Know?
The American robin shown here may be a true albino, since it appears to have a lack of pigmentation in the eyes, legs and bill—as well as in the distinct plumage.

Q For two years in a row, a white robin briefly showed up at my birdbath. How rare is it, and do you think it could be the same bird?

Susan Jacobsen
NEW BERLIN, WISCONSIN

Kenn and Kimberly: For some reason, the lack of pigment in the feathers—called leucism or albinism—seems to occur more often in robins than in most other birds. But it's still fairly rare, affecting about one out of every 30,000 robins, according to some estimates. So there's a good chance you saw the same bird twice, rather than two different ones. Individual robins tend to be faithful to certain locations, returning to the same places in summer, winter and even during migration, so it's possible that you might see your special visitor again.

Q I saw two orioles fighting, and after one flew away, the other one stayed upside down for about 10 minutes before eventually flying off. Any idea why he was in this odd position?

Doreen Wagner
BEAVERTOWN, PENNSYLVANIA

Kenn and Kimberly: Although some birds, like parrots, will regularly hang upside down, it's not normal for most songbirds to be in this position. We've seen it happen rarely, when the birds apparently were stunned. The male Baltimore oriole in your photo may have been dazed; perhaps the other bird pecked him hard on the head. The fact that he eventually righted himself and flew away probably means that he recovered all right. But it's unusual for a bird fight to get that rough.

Q I recently discovered this strange "frond ball" at the top of a fern in my shade garden. Can you tell me more about it?

Ruth Geraci SUMMERDALE, ALABAMA

Melinda: A close look at this photo reveals fine silky strands holding the fronds into the ball. My best guess is that an insect created this safe haven to lay eggs or pupate from its immature to mature stage (such as a caterpillar changing into a butterfly). If this happens again, keep an eye on the unique growth, and watch to see who exits this cozy home.

Fern Facts

Unlike most plants, ferns do not have seeds or flowers—instead, they reproduce by spores. Pair these funky-looking shade lovers with hostas, violas, bleeding hearts or lungwort for major textural appeal in your garden.

Q While looking for trilliums, I discovered this unusual bloom among the normal ones. What caused this? Can I expect it to happen again?

Rebecca Landwehr MATTOON, WISCONSIN

Melinda: What a wonderful surprise! There have been reports from a few lucky hikers who have found these in the wild. They are also for sale at a few specialty nurseries. It's not uncommon for plants to mutate or morph in response to the environment or pest damage or simply over time. Sometimes the change is permanent and other times it is not. Note the location and visit next year to see if this special trillium returns.

Did You Know?
Trilliums typically have three petals on top of three sepals and bloom in early spring.

Q This house finch visited my feeders. Something was wrong with one of its eyes. Do you know what the problem was?

Sonja Puhek
COLORADO SPRINGS, COLORADO

Kenn and Kimberly: This looks like a bacterial infection called conjunctivitis. It's often known as "house finch eye disease," but other finches suffer from it, too. Birds with conjunctivitis have swollen, crusty eyes, impairing their vision so that it's hard for them to find food and escape predators. The infection doesn't affect humans but can be contagious to other birds, so if the fliers at your feeders show symptoms, it's best to take the feeders down for a few days and clean them thoroughly. (Because the bird in your photo seems to have this condition in only one eye, it's possible that something else might be the cause.)

Q We saw these ducks while at the Sacramento National Wildlife Refuge Complex in October. What kind are they?

Roy and Debbie Pardee
UKIAH, CONNECTICUT

Kenn and Kimberly: The short answer is that these are escaped domestic ducks, but the long answer is more interesting. Most domestic ducks are descended from either mallards or Muscovy ducks, and those in your photo are in the mallard line. Over the last several centuries, people have developed many distinctive breeds of these ducks, ranging from all white to glossy greenish black, and many colors in between. These two look most similar to a rare breed called the Ancona duck, but they are not completely typical. When domestic ducks escape from captivity, they may wander in the wild for years, causing confusion for bird watchers.

Q Did this northern cardinal have a run-in with a predator or did disease cause his feathers to fall out?

Janinie Neiswender
ETTERS, PENNSYLVANIA

Kenn and Kimberly: It's fairly common to see cardinals looking like this in late summer or early fall when they go through the process of molt (growing a fresh set of feathers). Usually the feathers are replaced just a few at a time, but cardinals sometimes drop most of their head feathers at once. If the bird stays bareheaded for more than a couple of weeks, or if you see this at a completely different time of year, the affected cardinal might have a skin disease or an infestation of feather mites on its head.

Q I put my poinsettias in the garden during the summer and bring them indoors in fall. The blooms are changing colors. There were three blooms of different colors on one plant. What's going on?

Nancy Millar DUGSPUR, VIRGINIA

Melinda: First, congratulations on reblooming your poinsettias! That's quite an accomplishment. Changes in flower color like this are usually due to a mutation. Many popular new varieties develop as a result of hybridization or an attractive mutation that breeders discover and purposely propagate. Some of these plants will mutate (or revert) back to the original color, while others take on still another color. Enjoy the surprising variety and your gardening success.

Q This woodpecker visits our feeders. What species is it?

Scott and Jean DeGolier WAUNAKEE, WISCONSIN

Kenn and Kimberly: Every once in a while a birder is lucky enough to see a truly unique specimen; this is such a bird. It's a downy woodpecker, but one with an odd condition affecting its plumage. The feathers that ordinarily would be black are a light brownish gray, apparently because the melanin pigments in those feathers are reduced. In technical terms, this would be called either leucistic or dilute plumage. Although birds with odd-colored feathers look distinctly unusual, they often lead healthy lives, finding mates and raising young, just as most normally colored individuals do.

Perfectly Imperfect Plumage

Discover why birds develop surprising and irregular feather colors.

By Kenn and Kimberly Kaufman

A stunning sight, this black-chinned hummingbird is leucistic, which means it's missing pigments in its feathers.

Light and Lovely

Melanin pigments in this bald eagle's feathers are low, resulting in an appearance that's pale brown instead of dark brown.

SEEING BIRDS PARADE their colorful feathers is one of the greatest joys in watching winged visitors. The hues and patterns of the plumage can be both decorative and practical, making birds gaudy enough to attract mates or subtle enough to blend into their surroundings. Plumage is also a reliable way for bird-watchers to recognize different species.

Sometimes, though, a bird has a very unusual feather pattern—one that is not quite how it's supposed to look or doesn't match up with the pictures in the book. Such striking and surprising colors have a number of causes. If you know what makes these odd variations possible, it's exciting, not confusing, when you spot one.

Flashes of White

A flock of robins gather on the lawn and among them is a bird that looks similar, but with big patches of white. A flock of house sparrows flies past, and there's an all-white bird with them. Are they some rare visitors?

No, they're just individuals of the same kind that lack normal pigments in their feathers.

Most of the black, gray, brown and reddish brown tones in feathers are created by pigments called melanins. If these pigments are missing, feathers may grow in pure white. Birds might have just a few white feathers, large random spots of them—or they might look completely white. All of these individuals are known as leucistic. Their appearance may throw you off at first, but with careful study, you can identify most by their shape and behavior, and if they're flocking with others of their own kind.

Splotchy white birds are sometimes called partial albinos, but scientists disagree on whether this is a valid term. A true albino bird lacks all pigments, including in its eyes. So it would have white feathers and pink eyes (from blood vessels showing through). Genuine albinos rarely live long in the wild, so birders don't see them often. It's generally safe to assume that a white or partly white bird is leucistic.

A leucistic female northern cardinal shows some red, but the dark brown pigments are absent.

In contrast, while a lack of melanin leads to white feathers, it is also possible for birds to have an excess of dark pigment. Extra dark, or melanistic, individuals are fairly common in some hawk species, and it's part of their normal variation. For most songbirds, however, melanistic plumages are very rare.

A Range of Hues

Red, orange and yellow feathers are usually created by other kinds of pigments called carotenoids, which are often independent of melanins. So a leucistic red-winged blackbird might have white plumage where melanin is

A 1-year-old male indigo bunting has molted into spring plumage—a patchy mix of brown and blue feathers.

missing from the black feathers but still show typical red and yellow pigment in the wings.

Carotenoid colors often show odd variations, too, as in the rare male northern cardinals that are bright yellow instead of red.

Diet affects carotenoid pigments. For example, male house finches are usually bright red on the chest, but if they have a poor diet, their new feathers grow in orange and yellow. And if cedar waxwings eat the fruits from certain exotic plants, the tips of their tail feathers are known to turn red instead of the usual yellow.

Costume Change

Sometimes birds show unique color patterns for a while simply because they're changing from one set of feathers to another.

As a very general rule, a healthy wild bird replaces all its feathers at least once a year, just a few at a time, in a process called a molt. The new feathers are often the same colors as the ones they're replacing, so the effect isn't obvious. But some species change colors with the seasons, or as they become adults. When those birds are partway through the molt, they can look very

Balding Birds

If you've ever spotted a blue jay or a northern cardinal with a mostly bald head, the bird isn't sick—don't worry! It is simply suffering from tiny parasites that cause some feathers to fall out. Most birds survive and grow back a full head of feathers in a few weeks.

odd, with patterns unlike any picture in a field guide. Look for male American goldfinches to see an example of the process. In spring and fall they molt their head and body feathers, going from drab, buffy brown to brilliant gold and then back again. The process takes at least a couple of weeks and while it's happening, they wear a unique ever-changing coat of color.

Something similar happens with other birds that change with the seasons. Adult male indigo buntings are blue in summer, mostly brown in winter and a mix when they're in their first year

or in molt. Male scarlet tanagers trade their vibrant summer red for a winter costume of olive green, and they wear a mix of both in between. Adult male summer tanagers are bright red all year, but 1-year-old males are unevenly splotched as adult red starts to replace their baby olive.

Temporary Flair

Sometimes a bird sports unusual colors simply because birds are messy. They get into things and get discolored. It may be obvious, like when a wading bird has mud on its belly. But the stains come from their diet too. Birds feeding on ripe berries or small fruits may have a face stained blue, purple or black. Birds that prefer nectar can be dusted with flower pollen. It's common to see a hummingbird with tints of yellow or orange on its face where pollen has stuck to its feathers.

Whatever the cause for discoloration, some birds just don't follow the dress code. Finding such a unique individual is a highlight for anyone who loves the variety of birdlife.

Birds Out of Bounds

Surprised to spot birds off their usual course in the winter? Here's why.

By David Mizejewski

BIRDS SURPRISE US every single day. And every winter, we're bound to hear reports of birds showing up where they shouldn't be. For instance, tanagers, hummingbirds and others that fly south in winter are being spotted in some cold and snowy regions where they're not expected. Why this happens is often a mystery. It could be as simple as a young, inexperienced bird getting confused. Let's take a look at what could be going on.

Getting Off Course

Most birds naturally have the ability to navigate, and most species don't need to follow their parents to their wintering grounds. But while young birds use instinct to make these long journeys, on their first migration they're unaware of a specific goal or destination and can go off course.

Another explanation can be that a bird's internal navigation system is malfunctioning in some way, sending it off in the wrong direction.

Also, storms sometimes blow birds off course. Climate change is already affecting the migratory behavior of some species.

You can see an example of the unusual effects of climate change by looking at rufous hummingbirds. They've been spotted frequently in winter on the East Coast and in the Midwest during recent years. Eager birders on the East Coast keep their feeders out all winter in hopes that one of these rare guests makes an appearance. While researchers study why this is happening, birds continue to test out new breeding or wintering areas.

Understanding Migration

Sometimes reports of unexpected sightings result from nothing more than confusion about which species migrate and where they usually winter. Eastern bluebirds, for example, sometimes escape notice in the summer. So people can be puzzled to see them in the winter, not realizing that bluebirds in the southern part of their range are non-migratory and spend the winter in the same place they breed.

Whether you have a true vagrant or just a winter bird that surprises you, one thing is pretty certain: Leaving your feeders out will cause no harm. Don't worry that your food offerings are inviting out-of-season birds to stick around. Migration is triggered by several things, including seasonal changes in light, so a few feeders won't override the instinct. In fact, keeping feeders out can actually help these wayward birds survive the winter if they get stuck farther north than they should. They also give you a better chance at spotting a rarely seen bird right in your own backyard.

Ready To Share
Here's what to do when you see a rare bird.

- **Take a photo or video.** You'll want to remember the moment—and you'll get bragging rights, too!

- **Share it with a friend.** Call your best birder buddy over so he or she can also catch a glimpse of your fun find.

- **Report it.** Submit a report to eBird or other bird-tracking website.

Winter Wanderers
Do bluebirds belong in the North during winter? It depends. Some bluebirds migrate south for winter, while others settle into areas like the snowy Northeast.

Birdhouse Guidelines

Discover which dwellings are best for your backyard birds.

SPECIES	DIMENSIONS (LxWxH)	HOLE	PLACEMENT	COLOR	NOTES
Eastern bluebird	5"x5"x8"	1½" centered 6" above floor	5'-10' high in an open sunny area	light earth tones	likes open areas, especially facing a field
Tree swallow	5"x5"x6"	1½" centered 4" above floor	5'-8' high in the open; 50-100% sun	light earth tones or gray	within 2 miles of a pond or lake
Purple martin	multiple apartments 6"x6"x6"each	2⅛" centered 2¼" above floor	15'-20' high in the open	white	open yard without tall trees; near water
Tufted titmouse	4"x4"x8"	1¼" centered 6" above floor	4'-10' high	light earth tones	prefers to live in or near woods
Chickadee	4"x4"x8" or 5"x5"x8"	1⅛" centered 6" above floor	4'-8' high	light earth tones	small tree thicket
Nuthatch	4"x4"x10"	1¼" centered 7½" above floor	12'-25' high on tree trunk	bark-covered or natural	prefers to live in or near woods
House wren	4"x4"x8" or 4"x6"x8"	1" centered 6" above floor	5'-10' high on post or hung in tree	light earth tones or white	prefers lower branches of backyard trees
Northern flicker	7"x7"x18"	2½" centered 14" above floor	8'-20' high	light earth tones	put 4" of sawdust inside for nesting
Downy woodpecker	4"x4"x10"	1¼" centered 7½" above floor	12'-25' high on tree trunk	simulate natural cavity	prefers own excavation; provide sawdust
Red-headed woodpecker	6"x6"x15"	2" centered 6"-8" above floor	8'-20' high on post or tree trunk	simulate natural cavity	needs sawdust for nesting
Wood duck	10"x10"x24"	4"x3" elliptical 20" above floor	2'-5' high on post over water or 12'-40' high on tree facing water	light earth tones or natural	needs 3"-4" of sawdust or shavings for nesting
American kestrel	10'x10"x24"	4x3" elliptical 20" above floor	12'-40' high on post or tree trunk	light earth tones or natural	needs open approach on edge of woodlot or in isolated tree
Screech-owl	10"x10"x24"	4'x3" elliptical 20" above floor	12'-40' high on tree	light earth tones or natural	prefers open woods or edge of woodlot

Note: With the exception of wrens and purple martins, birds do not tolerate swaying birdhouses. Birdhouses should be firmly anchored to a post, a tree or the side of a building.

Chart source: *Garden Birds of America* by George H. Harrison. Willow Creek Press, 1996.

Birds and Their Favorite Foods

	Nyjer (thistle) seed	Cracked corn	White proso millet	Black oil sunflower seed	Hulled sunflower seed	Beef suet	Fruit	Sugar water (nectar)*
Rose-breasted grosbeak				•	•			
Black-headed grosbeak				•	•			
Evening grosbeak		•	•	•	•			
Northern cardinal		•	•	•	•		•	
Indigo bunting	•		•		•			
Eastern towhee	•	•	•	•	•			
Dark-eyed junco	•	•	•	•	•			
White-crowned sparrow	•	•	•	•	•			
White-throated sparrow	•	•	•	•	•			
American tree sparrow	•	•	•		•			
Chipping sparrow	•	•	•		•			
Song sparrow	•	•	•		•			
House sparrow	•	•	•		•			
House finch	•	•	•	•	•			
Purple finch	•	•	•	•	•			
American goldfinch	•	•	•	•	•			
Pine siskin	•	•	•	•	•			
Scarlet tanager							•	•
Western tanager							•	•
Baltimore oriole							•	•
Red-winged blackbird		•		•	•			
Eastern bluebird							•	
Wood thrush							•	
American robin							•	
Gray catbird							•	
Northern mockingbird							•	
Brown thrasher							•	
Ruby-throated hummingbird								•
Anna's hummingbird								•
Broad-tailed hummingbird								•
Tufted titmouse	•			•		•		
Black-capped chickadee	•			•	•	•		
White-breasted nuthatch				•	•	•		
Carolina wren						•		
Cedar waxwing							•	
Woodpecker				•	•	•	•	
Scrub-jay		•		•	•	•	•	
Blue jay		•		•	•	•	•	
Mourning dove	•	•	•					
Northern bobwhite		•	•		•			
Ring-necked pheasant		•	•		•			
Canada goose		•						
Mallard		•						

* To make sugar water, mix 4 parts water with 1 part sugar. Boil, cool and serve. Store leftovers in the refrigerator for up to a week. Change feeder nectar every 3 to 5 days.

Chart source: *Garden Birds of America* by George H. Harrison. Willow Creek Press, 1996.

Native Plants Chart

Attract more birds and butterflies by including native plants in your landscape.

	COMMON NAME	SCIENTIFIC NAME	HARDINESS ZONES	FLOWER COLOR	HEIGHT	BLOOM TIME	SOIL MOISTURE
DRY SOILS AND DRY CLIMATES (15"–25" ANNUAL PRECIPITATION)	Leadplant	*Amorpha canescens*	3-8	Purple	2'-3'	June-July	D, M
	Butterfly weed	*Asclepias tuberosa*	3-10	Orange	2'-3'	June-Aug.	D, M
	Smooth aster	*Aster laevis*	4-8	Blue	2'-4'	Aug.-Oct.	D, M
	Cream false indigo	*Baptisia bracteata*	4-9	Cream	1'-2'	May-June	D, M
	Purple prairie clover	*Dalea purpurea*	3-8	Purple	1'-2'	July-Aug.	D, M
	Pale purple coneflower	*Echinacea pallida*	4-8	Purple	3'-5'	June-July	D, M
	Prairie smoke	*Geum triflorum*	3-6	Pink	6"	May-June	D, M
	Dotted blazing star	*Liatris punctata*	3-9	Purple/Pink	1'-2'	Aug.-Oct.	D, M
	Wild lupine	*Lupinus perennis*	3-8	Blue	1'-2'	May-June	D
	Large-flowered beardtongue	*Penstemon grandiflorus*	3-7	Lavender	2'-4'	May-June	D
	Showy goldenrod	*Solidago speciosa*	3-8	Yellow	1'-3'	Aug.-Sept.	D, M
	Bird's-foot violet	*Viola pedata*	3-9	Blue	6"	Apr.-June	D
MEDIUM SOILS IN AVERAGE RAINFALL CLIMATES (25"–45" ANNUAL PRECIPITATION)	Nodding pink onion	*Allium cernuum*	3-8	White/Pink	1'-2'	July-Aug.	M, Mo
	New England aster	*Aster novae-angliae*	3-7	Blue/Purple	3'-6'	Aug.-Sept.	M, Mo
	Blue false indigo	*Baptisia australis*	3-10	Blue	3'-5'	June-July	M, Mo
	White false indigo	*Baptisia lactea*	4-9	White	3'-5'	June-July	M, Mo
	Shooting star	*Dodecatheon meadia*	4-8	White/Pink	1'-2'	May-June	M, Mo
	Purple coneflower	*Echinacea purpurea*	4-8	Purple	3'-4'	July-Sept.	M, Mo
	Rattlesnake master	*Eryngium yuccifolium*	4-9	White	3'-5'	June-Aug.	M
	Prairie blazing star	*Liatris pycnostachya*	3-9	Purple/Pink	3'-5'	July-Aug.	M, Mo
	Wild quinine	*Parthenium integrifolium*	4-8	White	3'-5'	June-Sept.	M, Mo
	Yellow coneflower	*Ratibida pinnata*	3-9	Yellow	3'-6'	July-Sept.	M, Mo
	Royal catchfly	*Silene regia*	4-9	Red	2'-4'	July-Aug.	M
	Stiff goldenrod	*Solidago rigida*	3-9	Yellow	3'-5'	Aug.-Sept.	M, Mo
MOIST SOILS AND MOIST CLIMATES (45"–60" ANNUAL PRECIPITATION)	Wild hyacinth	*Camassia scilloides*	4-8	White	1'-2'	May-June	M, Mo
	Tall Joe Pye weed	*Eupatorium fistulosum*	4-9	Purple/Pink	5'-8'	Aug.-Sept.	Mo, W
	Queen of the prairie	*Filipendula rubra*	3-6	Pink	4'-5'	June-July	M, Mo
	Bottle gentian	*Gentiana andrewsii*	3-6	Blue	1'-2'	Aug.-Oct.	Mo, W
	Rose mallow	*Hibiscus palustris*	4-9	Pink	3'-6'	July-Sept.	Mo, W
	Dense blazing star	*Liatris spicata*	4-10	Purple/Pink	3'-6'	Aug.-Sept.	Mo, W
	Cardinal flower	*Lobelia cardinalis*	3-9	Red	2'-5'	July-Sept.	Mo, W
	Marsh phlox	*Phlox glaberrima*	4-8	Red/ Purple	2'-4'	June-July	M, Mo
	Sweet black-eyed Susan	*Rudbeckia subtomentosa*	3-9	Yellow	4'-6'	Aug.-Oct.	M, Mo
	Ohio goldenrod	*Solidago ohioensis*	4-5	Yellow	3'-4'	Aug.-Sept.	M, Mo
	Tall ironweed	*Vernonia altissima*	4-9	Red/Pink	5'-8'	Aug.-Sept.	Mo, W
	Culver's root	*Veronicastrum virginicum*	3-8	White	3'-6'	July-Aug.	M, Mo

SOIL MOISTURE KEY

D = Dry (Well-drained sandy and rocky soils), **M** = Medium (Normal garden soils such as loam, sandy loam and clay loam),
Mo = Moist (Soils that stay moist below the surface, but are not boggy; may dry out in late summer),
W = Wet (Soils that are continually moist through the growing season, subject to short periods of spring flooding).

Grow for Your Zone

Find the number associated with your region,
and stick to plants that will thrive in your area.

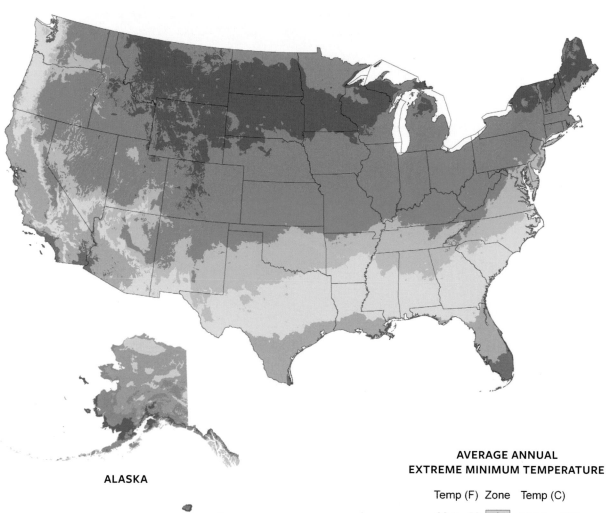

ALASKA

HAWAII

USDA PLANT HARDINESS ZONES

Hardiness zones reflect the average annual
minimum cold temperatures for an area. If it's
difficult to precisely locate your city on the map
above, use the interactive version on the USDA
website, *planthardiness.ars.usda.gov*. Enter your
ZIP code, then your hardiness zone and average
minimum winter temperature range will appear.

AVERAGE ANNUAL
EXTREME MINIMUM TEMPERATURE

Temp (F)	Zone	Temp (C)
-60 to -50	1	-51.1 to -45.6
-50 to -40	2	-45.6 to -40
-40 to -30	3	-40 to -34.4
-30 to -20	4	-34.4 to -28.9
-20 to -10	5	-28.9 to -23.3
-10 to 0	6	-23.3 to -17.8
0 to 10	7	-17.8 to -12.2
10 to 20	8	-12.2 to -6.7
20 to 30	9	-6.7 to -1.1
30 to 40	10	-1.1 to 4.4
40 to 50	11	4.4 to 10
50 to 60	12	10 to 15.6
60 to 70	13	15.6 to 21.1

Food Fight

I have a large grapevine wreath mounted over a platform
feeder on my deck, and on this particular day, the blue
jays seemed to be fighting a little more than usual over the
seed. One would be eating and another would fly in and
scare it off. The blue jay on the left hopped out of the way
a few times, but finally hunkered down, apparently
determined not to be bullied off the feeder.

Susan George AVOCA, MICHIGAN

Birds&Blooms